INSIGHT STUDIES

Insight Studies

A Practice-Based Approach to Self-Knowledge and Critical Thinking

KENNETH R. MELCHIN

UNIVERSITY OF TORONTO PRESS
Toronto Buffalo London

© University of Toronto Press 2025
Toronto Buffalo London
utppublishing.com

ISBN 978-1-4875-6610-4 (cloth)   ISBN 978-1-4875-6612-8 (EPUB)
                                   ISBN 978-1-4875-6611-1 (PDF)

Library and Archives Canada Cataloguing in Publication

Title: Insight studies : a practice-based approach to self-knowledge and critical thinking / Kenneth R. Melchin.
Names: Melchin, Kenneth R., 1949– author
Description: Includes bibliographical references and index.
Identifiers: Canadiana (print) 20250198045 | Canadiana (ebook) 20250198096 | ISBN 9781487566104 (cloth) | ISBN 9781487566111 (PDF) | ISBN 9781487566128 (EPUB)
Subjects: LCSH: Insight. | LCSH: Critical thinking. | LCSH: Self-knowledge, Theory of.
Classification: LCC BF449.5 .M45 2025 | DDC 153.4 – dc23

Cover design: Val Cooke and Will Brown
Cover image: CHOKDEEPERM/Shutterstock.com

We wish to acknowledge the land on which the University of Toronto Press operates. This land is the traditional territory of the Wendat, the Anishnaabeg, the Haudenosaunee, the Métis, and the Mississaugas of the Credit First Nation.

University of Toronto Press acknowledges the financial support of the Government of Canada, the Canada Council for the Arts, and the Ontario Arts Council, an agency of the Government of Ontario, for its publishing activities.

For Mike Payette, with thanks for your support, dedication, and excellent comments.

Contents

Preface ix

1 Introduction to Insight Studies   3
    Insight Studies: What Kind of Organism Am I?   4
    Self-Knowledge, Relationships, and Democracies   9
    Self-Knowledge and Critical Thinking   14
    A Practice-Based Approach   17
    Outline of the Chapters and Learning Modules   20

2 Getting Started: Practice Modules 1–3   24
    Selecting Puzzles That Are Right for You   25
    Module 1: Establishing a Daily Routine of Puzzle Solving   29
    Module 2: A Special Procedure for Puzzle Solving   31
    Excursus: Introducing Self-Knowing   36
    Module 3: Focusing on Your Mind's Operations   39
    Applying the Skills   43

3 Identifying the Operations: Practice Modules 4–6   46
    Module 4: Differentiating Groups of Operations   47
    Excursus: Some Observations on the Skill Development
       Process   51
    Excursus: Introducing the Theory of Knowing   53
    Module 5: Identifying the Operation of Direct Insight   56
    Module 6: Identifying the Operation of Judgment   59
    Applying the Skills   63

4 Feelings, Values, and Decisions: Practice Modules 7–9   65
    Module 7: Identifying Feelings and Values   66
    Excursus: Revisiting the Theory of Knowing   69
    Module 8: Feelings, Values, and Decisions   72
    Module 9: Observing an Inner Normativity   76
    Applying the Skills   79
5 Applications   83
    Ethics and Discernment   84
    Conflict and Insight   89
    Sociology and Everyday Arguments   93
    Psychology and Problem-Solving   95
    Philosophy and Self-Possession   98
    Politics and Spirituality   101
    Concluding Reflections   104
6 Afterword   105

Appendix   109

Notes   119

Bibliography   127

Index   133

Preface

You can't simply read this book!

Well, I suppose you can if you want. But if you simply read it, you won't be sampling what the book has to offer. You need to be thinking of this as similar to a book of scales and exercises for learning to play the violin. The nine learning modules in chapters 2–4 are like the notes you play over and over again as you practise the scales and exercises. The textual materials in chapters 2–4 offer explanations of the skills and techniques for practising the exercises. Chapter 1 offers something like an introduction to the instrument and some reasons for devoting the time and effort required by the method. Chapter 5 offers six snapshots of novel achievements that were made possible because the people learned the skills.

The nine learning modules are offered as an approach to critical thinking, and the skills you learn as you practise the exercises help you learn to think more critically. But the approach is novel because the skills also help you think more curiously, more creatively, more intelligently, and more responsibly. The operations you explore in this approach include not only logic, judgment, criticism, and argument, but also questioning, understanding, verifying, valuing, and cooperating. Moreover, the path you follow as you work through the learning modules is a path of self-knowledge. You do not simply read about the operations your mind performs; you discover them for yourself in the act of using your mind to solve puzzles.

The word "insight" in the title signals that the approach is based on the work of the philosopher Bernard Lonergan, whose major work is *Insight: A Study of Human Understanding*. The word "philosopher," however, should not frighten you. In order to learn what the book offers, you do not need a background in philosophy. All you need is the willingness to devote the time and effort to practising the skills. The recommended time commitment is thirty minutes daily, five days per week, for nine weeks. If you are following a shorter course that focuses more narrowly on either modules 1–3 or 1–6, the time commitment is likely reduced to either three or six weeks.

I have said you do not need a background in philosophy to learn what the book offers. But this does not mean the book is not helpful for philosophy. It is. It is also helpful for the fields of politics, conflict studies, psychology, ethics, and sociology. Chapter 5 offers a brief survey of six authors who make novel contributions to these fields because they have learned the skills. Scholars familiar with the term "insight" and the work of Lonergan are often found working in the fields of theology and religious studies. And others have applied the work of Lonergan to fields such as medicine, physics, nursing, environmental science, management, and economics. So, the book also points beyond this course to resources that could prove helpful for your own discipline or profession.

The book can be used as a text for a core curriculum course in critical thinking. But instructors who develop the skills will discover that a course based on the book can contribute to any course or program in any discipline. The learning modules lend themselves to both in-person and online learning formats. And the book can be used by self-help learners, particularly those who are innovative in finding online mentors or coaches who can offer help at crucial moments.

Because the method is practice-based, the book is short, the explanations are brief, and the focus is on the practice modules. To be sure, a host of questions will arise as learners work through the modules. The nature of these questions will differ depending on the fields and backgrounds of learners. Here is where the assistance of instructors proves helpful. In addition, I suggest consulting a companion text that offers more lengthy discussions of Lonergan's work. I recommend Patrick Byrne's book *The Ethics of Discernment*, particularly chapters 1–3. In the notes to the chapters, I refer learners to other works that can help at various points along the way. Readers will observe that the final chapter of the book is not a summary chapter. This, again, is because the book's focus is on practice-based learning. My hope would be that learners come away from the course knowing how to *do something*, not simply *argue something*.

Learners will observe that chapter 5 is different from all the other chapters of the book. In a sense, you could say it is more like an appendix offering six illustrations of the self-knowing skills at work in six different disciplines. There is a disconnect between the line of questioning pursued in chapter 1 and the diverse lines of questioning pursued by the six authors. I tried to connect them but found that I could not. Still, there is indeed a link between these works and the line of exploration pursued here, and there is a reason why these authors have been selected. The six authors (a) carry Lonergan's work beyond the field of theology, where he situated most of his work, and (b) focus on the *practice* of self-knowing and not simply on theoretical aspects of Lonergan's work. These two concerns are central to this book. In addition, their works focus on life skills, and this is a central thread running through all the book's chapters. My hope is that learners will find that the contributions of the six authors make up for whatever loose ends you might find.

I would like to add one final comment before moving on to the acknowledgments. The authors selected for chapter 5 are all white and none are obvious in representing non-dominant perspectives. This is worth calling attention to and attempting to explain. My hope is that other authors will build on this approach and develop practice-based texts in Insight studies that reflect more diverse perspectives.

By way of explanation, let me say that the field of authors who carry Lonergan's work beyond theology and who focus not simply on his theory but on the practice of self-knowing is quite small. Normally, this could warrant accepting a less-than-ideal representation of non-dominant perspectives. That being said, a third of the authors are women, one author self-identifies as a member of the LGBTQ+ community, one author has published two books on Sargent Shriver that highlight his campaign against racism, and one author has devoted his career to teaching in a college whose mission includes outreach to minority groups in New York City. Considering, once more, the small size of this community of experts, the authors selected here do make reasonable progress towards representing non-dominant perspectives.

This book would not have been possible without the help of a large number of people: friends, mentors, colleagues, family, and students. Thanks to all of you. I began working with practice-based approaches to self-knowing when I first studied Lonergan at Concordia University, Montreal, in the late 1970s. I am grateful to Sean McEvenue for introducing me to Lonergan and to Phil McShane for introducing me to the practice-based approach. When I arrived at Saint Paul University, I was assigned a course entitled "Moral Existence," and I taught this course almost every year throughout my career. I wish to thank all the students who took this course. My approach involved an introduction to self-knowledge and an application to the field of ethics. Along the way, thanks to you, I learned a great deal about teaching self-knowing and critical thinking.

During my earlier years at Saint Paul University, I recall working with puzzles with Peter Monette, Paul Lewis, and Jean-Louis Munn in a reading course on Lonergan. Thanks to the three of you for your insights and your patience with my limited abilities. In the decades since then, many colleagues, students, and professionals participated in various sessions of the Lonergan Reading Group and in various research group sessions in which, from time to time, we employed the puzzle approach. I have compiled a list of names, and I am grateful to all of you for your interest, intelligence, and patience: Darlene O'Leary, Pierre Laviolette, Jessie MacNeill, Morag McAleese, Danny Lyonnais, Cheryl Picard, Neil Sargent, Derek Melchin, Anne Buchanan, Marnie Jull, Allison Hewitt, Natalie Dupuis, Colleen Currie, Tim Ragan, Amy Pauley, Susan Gray, Tom Grainger, Marilyn Martin van Beeck, Brian Tansey, Mercedes Kirchberg, John McKennirey, Kathleen Stevenson, Tom McAuley, and Elisabeth Nicholson. I fear I may have missed some names. If so, I apologize.

As I developed the practice-based approach, I was supported by numerous learners who were willing to assist in "road testing" the modules. With your help I was able to learn from my mistakes and refine the modules at each step along the way. My learning began in various sessions of the Lonergan Reading Group, with various members from the group mentioned above. I am also grateful to the students of my course THO 3172, "Faith and Contemporary Culture," offered at Saint

Paul University in the fall term, 2018. The course had a "Philosophical Practice" component, and your input helped me considerably. I thank the participants in the Glengarry Encore Education course, "Ethics of Bernard Lonergan," offered in the winter term, 2019. You were enthusiastic and gracious in participating in the practice-based components. In the fall of 2019 and the winter-spring term of 2020, I was fortunate to work with an amazing group of conflict practitioners in two online Insight courses: Kenneth Markeley, Cathy Campbell, Ian Forgeron, Shirley Wallace, Cheryl Picard, Beth Nicholson, and Catherine Ali. The courses were online adaptations of learning modules I had developed previously. My thanks go out to all of you.

Fred Lawrence, Director of the Lonergan Workshop at Boston College, was gracious in inviting me to present my work on Insight studies in a paper entitled "Lonergan and the Catholic University" at the 2017 Lonergan Workshop. And I am grateful to Patrick Byrne and Jeremy Wilkins, past and present directors of the Lonergan Institute at Boston College, for your continued support for my work. My dear friends and colleagues on the board of directors of the Lonergan Research Institute at the University of Toronto have been unwavering in their support for my work, and for this I am grateful. I thank the leadership team at Insight Collaborations International (ICI), notably Megan Price, Marnie Jull, Vieve Price, and Norah Wardell, for inviting me to present my work as part of an Insight Discussion Group panel in June 2023. And I thank my colleagues, Mike Stebbins, Paul LaChance, Richard Grallo, Jamie Price, and Rob De La Noval, for inviting me to join you in our Insight Studies Roundtable session presented online, in April 2024, via the "Insight Today" website www.insighttodayonline.com.

I wish to thank Art Marvin, husband of my cousin Donna, who was the nearby friend and tree expert in my story in chapter 1. I will always remember that day we went walking together in our back bush. Over the years, my family has been generous and long-suffering in listening to my lectures and rants on the topic of Insight studies. My thanks go out to you: Derek and Sarah, Nick and Naomi, Pat and Julie, Mike and Rosemary, Mike and Robin, Jim and Donna, Marilyn and Butch. I am grateful to Maïa Bianchi Melchin, Solanne Bianchi Melchin, and Chris Melchin for reading sections of chapters, offering comments, and engaging in discussion.

I wish to thank my Saint Paul University colleagues, Jim Pambrun, Cathy Clifford, Mark Slatter, and Hazel Markwell, for your support for my work in Lonergan studies. And I wish to thank the Saint Paul University administration for your support for the work of The Lonergan Centre through the years. Special thanks go out to Elisabeth Nicholson, who has taken on the role of director of the Lonergan Centre. Your understanding and dedication are remarkable.

I am indebted to three friends and colleagues, Cheryl Picard, Morag McAleese, and Jamie Price, for working with me over the years in exploring and applying self-appropriation to the fields of peace and conflict studies and workplace ethics. And I am indebted to three friends and colleagues, Mike Stebbins, Richard Grallo, and Paul LaChance, for your ongoing help and support in my practice-based work in Insight studies. I am grateful to Andrea Bartoli for your many years of support for our application of Insight to the field of conflict.

My thanks and appreciation go out to Daniel Quinlan of the University of Toronto Press for taking on this book project and guiding me through the steps to publication. I am grateful to the readers who provided helpful comments on the manuscript for UTP. It was a pleasure to receive contributions from Perrin Lindelauf, Leah Connor, and Matthew MacLellan during the copyediting, indexing, and page proof stages. To be sure, I take sole responsibility for any errors or faults that remain in the final text. But I can say that the book is improved significantly because of the help you provided.

Early in my research, my work on self-appropriation and its applications was supported by a grant from the Social Sciences and Humanities Research Council of Canada, 2004–7. Further research on the application of Lonergan to the field of peace and conflict studies was supported by The Sargent Shriver Peace Institute. This volume was published with the aid of a grant from the Aid to Scholarly Publications Program of the Canadian Federation for the Humanities and Social Sciences.

My thanks go out to my wife, Sandie, for your friendship and support through the many years of this project. I am doubly grateful to you for loaning me your brother, Mike Payette, to whom this book is dedicated. At one point, when my spirits were flagging, Mike provided the interest and support needed for me to keep going. You were willing to devote the time and effort to practising the modules, and at every step along the way, your excellent comments helped me in revising and improving the manuscript. Thanks, Mike!

INSIGHT STUDIES

CHAPTER ONE

Introduction to Insight Studies

In our studies, relationships, and workplaces, we use tools. These days, the obvious tools are computerized devices. The most important tool we use, however, is not so obvious: it is our minds. In fact, this is the tool we use to develop all the other tools, and it is the tool we use to control the way we use all the other tools. You may be curious about the expression, "Insight studies." The straightforward response is this: using your mind properly requires learning how it works and practice in using it properly. Insight studies offers skills for helping you do this.

Think about coffee makers and airplanes. If you buy a coffee maker, it likely comes with an instruction manual. You may end up reading the manual or you may not. Either way, the stakes are not very high if you do not use it properly. You may get bad-tasting coffee, you may even get an electric shock, but unless you do something really foolish, the consequences of not using it properly are not too serious.

Not so with airplanes. If you buy an airplane and do not learn how it works or practise using it properly, using it will likely harm you. Your mind is more like an airplane than a coffee maker. If you do not learn how it works or practise using it properly, it will likely harm you. Perhaps just as important, it will likely harm those around you, those you love. I would say this is worth pondering.

INSIGHT STUDIES: WHAT KIND OF ORGANISM AM I?

Instead of starting out with a detailed definition of Insight studies, I would like to tell you a story about something that happened to me. It is a story about an important step in my own journey of self-knowing. My story involves an experience that led me to ask the question: what kind of organism am I? I do not know whether you have ever asked yourself this question. But it is worth considering. It ended up changing me in ways that have proven to be quite strange and thrilling.

In graduate school, I had learned something about the work of the Canadian philosopher Bernard Lonergan, and I was impressed with what I had learned.[1] His method invites us to catch ourselves in our acts of understanding. When we do this, we discover that our minds have an ordered structure that we can learn to observe. As we develop and practise the skills for observing this structure, we gain the ability to make decisions to stop thinking and acting in ways that bring us into conflict with ourselves. I had learned about the philosophical implications of this work but had yet to discover how to practise his method in daily living.[2] What I would discover in the years following was that practising the method in everyday life can change the way I think and feel about myself and my relations with the living things around me.

After graduating, I started teaching at Saint Paul University in Ottawa. We had a young family and were fortunate to be able to build a house in the country outside of Ottawa. Soon after moving in, I began noticing that I was not surrounded by pavement and buildings. Rather, I was surrounded by living things, things that move themselves. I grew up in the city where things stay put when you set them down, so when I first moved out here, I did not notice that the things around me were alive; they did not stay put.

The living thing whose capacity for self-movement first caught my attention did so when it frightened me. Oddly enough, it was not one of the wild animals whose habitat we had appropriated. Rather, it was the field around our house. We had bought a piece of property and arranged to have a house built. Like many young couples at the time, we pinched our pennies and built a house that stretched our budget, so after paying the mortgage and feeding the family, we were not left with much. To build the house, we had paid a sizeable amount of money to have the brush cleared. We thought we could keep this cleared by using an inexpensive lawn mower built for the city.

Ha! What a joke! What we discovered was that our field was alive! It moved itself. Most important, it did so rapidly, relentlessly, and powerfully. It quickly overwhelmed the capacities of our little city lawn mower and its owner. Eventually, through costly trial and error, we learned that the price tag of a machine that was a match for the self-moving capacity of our field was $11,000. This was when $11,000 was a lot more money than it is today. This frightened me. Actually, it was not just the money that frightened me; it was the fact that the field did not care about the money, it kept on growing back rapidly, relentlessly, powerfully. The only thing that could stop it was a lot of money we did not have.

What attracted my attention was the self-moving capacity of our field. Our field was alive. To be sure, the money was what first got my attention. But once jolted out of complacent ignorance, I became curious. What is this life that surrounds us? So, I decided to learn more about our field with its self-moving capacity. A nearby friend was a tree expert, so one day he took me walking through the field behind our house.

I kept a small part of our field cut with the machine I had at the time. Of course, the key word is "small." Even when I got a proper machine, my capacity for keeping our living field cut remained rather limited. So, I made peace with our field and drew a line beyond which it could grow happily wild. Beyond this line, we could walk until we came to a stand of trees we called "the bush." Beyond the bush, we knew we had six acres of mosquito-infested swamp. These days we grace this sort of thing with the dignified title of "wetland." Of course, this, too, is very much alive, but I was not to learn about this until later.

I recall the day I walked through our wild field with my friend. He kept talking about our trees. Of course, I was looking forward as I walked, and the obvious trees were those standing far away at the end of the field, the bush that occupied the piece of property between our open field and our swamp. I was amazed at his ability to tell me what kinds of trees we had. They were so far away. How could he see them? How could he identify them at this distance? So I asked. He stopped and looked at me. He told me he wasn't talking about *those* trees, he was talking about *these* trees. "What trees?" I asked. "The ones growing here at your feet," he said. The way he looked at me, I felt like a fool. Thankfully, he chuckled. So, I stopped looking forward and started looking down. What I learned was that things that look like grass are not necessarily grass. They can be trees. I was amazed. In the years following, I learned a lot about the trees that do not look like trees.

Since that day, I have learned a few things, not just about trees, but about myself. The first was that I began thinking differently about myself.[3] I began thinking about myself as an organism among other organisms. As long as I lived in a city, it was easy to neglect this line of thought. I suppose it was partly because I did not have much with which to compare myself. But I think the thing that struck me was that organisms have a life pattern and inner structure to them, and this pattern and structure are not put there by humans. In fact, they unfold and flourish without any help from humans. It is a structure that makes them live and act the way they do. I suppose I was used to things like technological devices that have an inner structure because humans put it there. What I began to learn in earnest was that living organisms have an inner structure that is not put there by humans. I began wondering about my own inner structure, which was not put there by humans. If I, too, am an organism, then what kind of organism am I?

Perhaps you can appreciate how this question gained significance for me. Here in the country, if you pay careful attention, you can notice that organisms have an inner structure that is remarkably dynamic. They are born, they are cared for in some way within some ecological niche, they reach out to find the food and water they need, they reach out to find the warmth and sunlight they need, they grow through various stages of adolescence into adulthood, they give birth to offspring, they self-organize into communities with other organisms that are both like and unlike them, they provide their own forms of care for their offspring until they can survive on their own, they adapt to survive through the onslaught of cold winters, they fight off diseases and parasites, they genetically mutate through the generations to adapt to changing circumstances, they eventually begin aging and dying, and when they die, their bodies decompose to give both life and wonderful ecological niches to the generations that come after. Noticing these things takes time. For me, this dynamic inner structure was quite remarkable. Perhaps I too have some sort of dynamic inner structure?

As I thought about my relationship with the living things around me, I began noticing how curious I was about our living field. Here is where the work of Lonergan began shaping my path of self-knowledge.[4] Even more amazing than our field was my own curiosity about it. I just could not let it go! I could not stop wondering! What is this? What is going on? How does it work? What is the difference between this and that? Reflecting back on these events, I learned as much about my own curiosity and wonder as I did about our living field. My inner structure does not operate only on the organic level. It also operates on the level of my consciousness.[5] My consciousness is dynamized by curiosity and wonder. These, more than anything, provided keys for answering my question about what kind of organism I am. My discovery was that I am an organism with a curious mind and an inclination towards wonder. I am an organism that asks questions, gets insights, seeks verification, and makes decisions.

I have walked through these fields for decades with children and grandchildren, and I can assure you, I am not alone in this. Their minds have this same inner structure that none of us created. If we make a contribution to our self-creation, it is by using this structure, not by authoring it. Of course, as parents and teachers, we can do things to stifle it. But in this respect, we are sort of like the dogwoods, a tree that grows in our wild field. They secretly grow runners underground and then pop up new trees in favourable places farther away. Curiosity is like that. When we stifle it, the structure keeps moving underground and popping up somewhere else. Often it pops up as a remarkably innovative strategy for resisting us or getting back at us. Our minds are structured, and curiosity is the mover. It is a structure that propels us in our living and learning. Like other organisms, we are carried along a distinctive path of acting, living, and relating to others by this structure, and we are directed by its operation.

Thinking back about that day with my friend, there was another thing that struck me. This was about critical thinking.[6] As we walked through the field, we both could see, but only he could think critically. To me, all the grasses at my feet looked the same. To him, there were important differences, and he knew exactly what these differences meant. He was able to see, but he was also able to understand the differences. He was able to observe intelligently, gain insights, and verify his understanding to achieve objective factual knowledge. I, on the other hand, could not.

He could do this because he had learned the practice of critical thinking in this domain, and I had not. He had practised using his mind properly with this body of data. He had practised for many years. Trees have a structure to them that can be learned, but this learning takes practice over time. The structure of trees is not static; it is dynamic. Its growth stages are patterned so that some observable characteristics are discernible in early growth stages, but very different characteristics must be noted in later stages. It takes a trained mind to observe these characteristics, and this skill development takes time and requires accompanying trees through their stages of development and decline. In the years that followed, I spent countless hours practising these skills, not only in this field of experience, but in many others.

So, I have told you my story. Actually, you will notice I have told you two stories. The first is about my adventures learning about the living things around our house, the things that move themselves. But the second is the story of my learning about myself. It is the second story that is important for this book. The reason is that, like the field around our house, your mind also has an inner structure that moves itself.

Insight studies is a practice in which we discover and verify this inner structure by catching ourselves in the act of using our minds. In doing so, we notice things we had not noticed previously. We discover that our minds are as strange and spectacular as the other living things around us. As we gain and verify insights into how our minds work, we can learn how to use our minds more carefully, more critically, and more responsibly.

Insight studies is a discipline that teaches skills for self-knowledge and critical thinking, skills for helping answer the question: what kind of organism am I? The key word is "skills." Insight studies requires developing and practising skills for catching ourselves in the act of performing what scholars call "cognitional operations."[7] These are the familiar operations of questioning, observing, understanding, verifying, and deciding. The goal is learning how these operations work and how they work together. It is like learning a musical instrument. It requires starting at the beginning, daily practice, and a structured method in which early skills, once developed, lay down the basis for later skills. The upshot of this skill development is a capacity for thinking critically that can prove helpful in school, relationships, and workplaces.

SELF-KNOWLEDGE, RELATIONSHIPS, AND DEMOCRACIES

I have said that Insight studies can prove helpful in school, relationships, and workplaces. As you work with the modules, you will likely gain your own insights. Also, chapters 2, 3, and 4 conclude with short sections with suggestions for "Applying the Skills." For the present, let me offer some preliminary reasons for considering a practice-based program for self-knowledge and critical thinking. Why bother with this? How could this effort prove helpful? There is a time commitment involved: why would this time commitment be worthwhile? I will answer by saying a few words about relationships: first, the familiar relationships of personal and family life, and second, our relationships as citizens of democracies. Chapter 5, "Applications," offers six short surveys of other works that provide additional answers to these questions.

I am a musician and I play the bass. I first learned the violin playing classical music, and I learned the bass in rock and roll bands in high school. Through my adult life, I have been playing in jazz bands, both big and small. Much of the time I have played with musicians who are much better than me. If you are a bass player, you do most of your important learning in relationships. For me, playing music provided a context for gaining insights into relationships that have proven helpful in other areas of life.

Early on, I realized the bass is not an instrument you play very much alone. For one thing, it drives my partner crazy. For another, when played alone, it loses a lot of its appeal because it does not really sound like music. If you are not a jazz lover, you likely find bass solos the least pleasant parts of the tunes. To be sure, you have to do some practising alone. But the thing about the bass is what you learn while playing with others. In jazz, the bass player has an enormous effect on the band. You have to learn how to adjust your playing in light of this effect. You have to learn in relationships.

If you are inclined to love power, then be a bass player. I warn you though, your power only works when it enhances cooperation. It only works when you discern a groove that is emerging and work with it. When you try anything else, you find yourself powerful, but only powerful at wrecking things. Good musicians can spot this a mile away, and pretty soon you are out. As a bass player, you have to listen and discern, and this means cultivating the skills for discernment. Most important, it requires learning these skills while you are playing.

When I first started playing jazz, I was a hotshot. Those were the days when jazz-rock bassists were playing complex syncopated lines. I learned some of this, and I used to love showing off. I got my first regular jazz gig in a club with a seasoned pro. He loved my abilities but hated when I used them to show off. I would not listen; I just did my own thing. I learned a lot from him, the hard way.

I will spare you the details. But I will tell you that I learned about myself. I learned that the most important thing you can do as a bass player is this: listen carefully, understand exactly what the other musicians are intending, then work with these intentions to gather, support, assess, and enhance them, not in the direction you would like, but in the musically excellent direction emerging in the cooperation among them. Playing jazz is musical cooperation. It requires a great deal of technical knowledge about music. But it requires careful discernment of what is emerging in the way all the musicians are using this knowledge together.

I have found the self-knowledge I gained from music to be helpful in relationships. The learning that is the focus of Insight studies is this sort of thing. It is the learning of listening carefully, understanding what others are intending, and working with these intentions to support, assess, and enhance a direction towards excellence that is emerging in the common project. Doing this requires self-knowledge and the type of critical thinking that emphasizes insights and good judgments.

In relationships, we use our minds, and we are free to use our minds however we choose. This can be wonderful. But it can also be disastrous. This is because in relationships we often do not understand what is going on, and we fail to notice that we do not understand. When we do not use our minds properly, we do not notice we have misunderstood. We hold convictions, and one of them is that we've understood exactly what they're saying and doing. Social media magnifies this problem.

The fact is, however, other people are often different in ways I have failed to understand, and I have not noticed this failure. Moreover, their differences are not minor; they are major. They value things differently and do things I find threatening.[8] To discern properly, I must ask questions differently, I must gain new insights, I must make judgments and decisions that push me out of my comfort zone. This means using my mind differently. And I can do this better by gaining the self-knowledge that focuses on my mind's operations. This is the path of self-knowledge we follow in Insight studies.

Insight studies can also prove helpful in the relationships that are thrust upon us as citizens of democracies. Since the turn of the century, citizens of the West have watched our nations engage in wars in the name of democracy. On the home front, we have pondered the legacy of protesters storming the US Capitol dynamized by ideas about democracy. We seem to have no shortage of passion about democracy. Yet analyses of approaches reveal considerable disagreement about what democracy is and what it requires from us.[9] Reviewing these analyses, what stands out is both the fervour of our commitment and our confusion about what we have committed to. Perhaps democracy is something like our intimate relationships: our enthusiasm seems inversely proportionate to our grasp of what we've taken on.

Early on, I learned that democracy involves institutions. In a democracy, governments are elected, and their role is to assure the freedom and equality of citizens. The elected government's role is to protect my freedom and deal with the problems that arise when another person's exercise of freedom impinges on mine.[10] What I learned more recently, however, is that these ideas, as important as they are, do not get to the bottom of things.[11] We need to think, not just about institutions for freedom and equality, but about what we do with our freedom and equality. We need to think about our roles and responsibilities as citizens in democracies. For institutions to work, we need to be doing something important. Also, there are important things in democracy that are not done by institutions; they are done only by us as citizens. This requires that we use our minds wisely.

Throughout history, a variety of traditions have emerged to influence the way we think about democracy. One of these was launched by the Greeks and taken up again in later centuries. In this tradition, the starting point is not freedom and equality, but discussion and debate.[12] In this tradition, the focus is on citizens' participation in the conversations and debates that lead to decisions about how we will live together in society. Contrary to empires, oligarchies, monarchies, and totalitarian states, democracies do not simply impose these decisions on citizens. Rather, in one way or another, citizens themselves participate in discussion and debate about matters of public life. In elections, we pick leaders who represent our values and convictions. But we expect them to do this by carrying forward this practice of discussion and debate with us and with others on our behalf. The focus in this tradition is on discussing together how we will live together.

This resonates with ideas and convictions many of us hold. We are staunch believers that governments must not simply impose their ideas on us. Rather, we must be part of the process. In some way, our ideas need to be represented in policies and programs. The trouble, though, is that these ideas need to be workable in real life. They need to be thought through, not just by us, but by others. They must be assessed and verified. Our ideas about living together must reflect factual knowledge and reliable values.[13] This requires discussion with people who have relevant experience and expertise. It requires discussion and debate with others who hold different and conflicting convictions. How will we do this?

To answer, a group of political philosophers developed an approach that placed this focus on discussion and debate at the centre of their thinking about democracy. Instead of starting with freedom and equality, they started with discussion and debate. Their focus was on the social process of discussion itself, and they called it "deliberative democracy."[14] To respect the principles of freedom and equality, they argued that the procedures of discussion must guard against the oppressive use of power.

For discussion to be democratic, it must be open and free from domination. What this implies, however, is something we have not wanted to pronounce too loudly because it makes us uncomfortable. It means our discussion needs to be governed by rules and obligations that must command the agreement of all. In one way or another, the obligations governing democratic discussion must be universal. They cannot be different or diverse. They cannot be left to the freedom of individuals. They have to be the same for everyone. They have to be compatible with and find a home within the traditions, cultures, philosophies, and religions of all who would commit to democracies. Moreover, citizens must comply with these rules and obligations. Here's where respect for diversity and difference stops. Here's where respect for individual freedom stops. Here's where we must be the same! Oh dear!

Some philosophers have tried to wrestle with this discomfort by drawing a line between the obligations governing the discussion process and the obligations associated with the issues themselves. This approach has been called "discourse ethics."[15] The hope was that, even if people could not agree on the issues, if we agreed on the rules for the discussion process, we would have grounds for accepting the outcomes of discussions when they go against our wishes.

The problem, however, is that parties in the discussion process focus resolutely on the issues. The Canadian philosopher Charles Taylor has argued that an adequate understanding of democracy cannot avoid facing the challenge presented by the content of issues themselves. In my judgment, he is right. He concludes that the democratic process demands a lot from citizens. It requires that we work through our differences together. It requires rising above the divisions created by cultures, religions, and ideologies. It requires that we do this by reaching back into our own traditions and finding resources that can take us beyond our traditions. This must be done by all of us together as persons and citizens. Democracy requires discussion on how we will live and act together in society. And this discussion must be an authentic interpersonal engagement in which "we have been transformed by the study of the other."[16]

If you are reading carefully, you will notice this is no longer simply academic jargon. This is getting personal! Taylor is saying that if I am in a conflict with you about politics, *I have to be willing to be transformed by the study of you?* ... Hmmm ... I can tell you that when I am in a conflict, this is the last thing I want. Yet this is indeed what democracy requires of me. I have to learn to do this. I have to learn to want this. This means I have to practise it.

Learning from others amid the conflicts of democratic discussion requires growth in self-knowledge. This is because such learning involves transformative experiences, experiences that change us, and we need to learn how to navigate these changes.[17] These transformations are often difficult and unpleasant. They involve the emergence into consciousness of new elements that, at first, are strange and unfamiliar. They make us uncomfortable. They require learning to appreciate values we've not cared about previously, values we find threatening. They require changing our priorities. Our learning involves cultivating new habits of caring and feeling. All of this requires self-knowledge.

Eventually, when verified, this learning proves to be worth it. It gives rise to broader horizons, new frameworks for understanding, new and better standards for evaluation and judgment.[18] Democratic discussion requires this transformative learning in the midst of conflicts. This places the idea of self-knowledge at the heart of our thinking about democracy. Most importantly, it requires self-knowledge of the operations involved in the transformative learning that occurs in democratic discussion.[19]

SELF-KNOWLEDGE AND CRITICAL THINKING

Insight studies offers a practice-based method for identifying and investigating our own operations of questioning, experiencing, understanding, verifying, and deciding. It does not require that learners accept a culture, religion, or philosophy. It only requires that we devote the time and effort to developing the required skills. In personal life and as citizens, our challenges arise in relationships, often in the midst of conflicts. We must learn from others we do not like. Even when we must learn from others we do like, it is often in the midst of conflicts when we like them least. This method helps us understand the operations involved in this learning. It helps us know ourselves better so we can use these operations more critically, more responsibly.

Insight studies is offered as a self-knowledge approach to critical thinking. And so a few words are in order about critical thinking. Psychologist Richard Grallo has argued that approaches to critical thinking generally focus on the operations of judgment and decision.[20] He finds this focus helpful but overly narrow. This is because, when we are careful in observing our critical thinking, particularly when we are problem-solving, we find that our minds move back and forth among a much wider range of operations that includes questioning, insight, and social trust. These operations must also be investigated and understood. In fact, understanding questioning and insight can change our understanding of what's involved in judgment and decision. He finds that even when we perform the operations of judgment and decision, we do so within three distinct patterns that are affected by the types of questions we have posed and the types of insights we have gained. Grallo's point is that programs in critical thinking need to include the self-investigation methods that can help us understand and verify the full range of our minds' operations.

The key to the Insight approach is the method for investigating our minds' operations. The important word here is "method." Using a method, I can discover things for myself. I can verify them for myself. I can observe that the ideas are not simply about someone else, they are about me. They help me answer my own question: what kind of organism am I? I do not have to simply accept someone else's opinion or pronouncement. I can learn for myself that these things are true about me.

You may be thinking: what if my mind's operations are different from someone else's? This is a really good question. My answer is that there are indeed individual style differences. But let me point out something interesting. When women and men from the sciences explain differences, they do so by developing explanatory frameworks that identify common elements that relate and combine in diverse ways.[21] The diversity that results from these frameworks, when verified, is often far more extensive than anything we'd imagined previously. But the key to explaining diversity is discovering the fundamental commonalities, the elements and relationships shared by all.

If you have thought recently about buying a car, for example, you have likely observed that, with electric vehicles, the challenge of choosing wisely has become more difficult. The variety of types, technologies, makes, and models appears endless. Each year, new innovations and new models come to market, and the diversity seems to increase year by year. Notice, however, that if I were to ask you about this diversity, if you knew something about cars, you would answer by pointing out different types of drive technologies, different types of engines, different types of fuels, different types of batteries, different types of transmissions, different types of suspensions, different types of traction controls, different types of computerized devices, and different body types. You would speak about the differences by speaking about things shared in common: drive technologies, engines, fuels, batteries, transmissions, suspensions, traction controls, computerized devices, and body types. Your explanation of differences would be an explanation of different types and arrangements of things held in common.

Investigating critical thinking involves a similar approach. If we are to learn about our own distinctive ways of thinking, we can only do so by first understanding a basic underlying structure of operations that is shared by everyone. Once we get clear on this, our explanatory framework, if it proves correct, provides tools for explaining the considerable diversity we find in the various ways these operations combine in our thinking styles. This is the interesting thing about science. Insights into common elements and relations provide the basis for explaining diversity and difference.

You may not feel comfortable with this idea. So, if we were in a face-to-face conversation, you would likely challenge my claim. If you did, I would not point to the content of your statement. Rather, my response would be to point to the act you just performed, the act of challenging. My response would be: yes of course! A challenge is a decision based on a judgment. Decision and judgment are two of the mind's basic operations that are shared by everyone. If you were to appeal to evidence to show you were right, then my response would be: yes of course! Appealing to evidence in support of a judgment is another basic operation that is shared by everyone. If you were to say that I have not understood you, then I would say: you are right! Perhaps I need to gain a new insight. Insight is another operation in the basic structure that is shared by everyone.

The fact is, in objecting, you would be using the very operations I am proposing we explore.[22] Moreover, you would implicitly but forcefully appeal to me to use these operations properly. You would know that having a conversation with me requires that we both use these operations critically and responsibly. Otherwise, you know the conversation would be a waste of your time and mine. To be sure, you have not formulated any of these obligations in words. But if you examine your behaviour carefully, you will notice that these obligations are operative in the background of your mind, as expectations you impose on both of us in the conversation. You expect me to be a careful and responsible interlocutor. This is what I mean by a basic structure of operations that we all hold in common.

Insight studies is a self-knowledge approach to critical thinking in which we develop and practise the skills for investigating the operations of our minds. Regardless of whether we have observed these operations, we can be sure they have exercised an enormous influence in our lives. They still do. Bernard Lonergan has called this activity of discovering and appropriating our minds' operations "self-appropriation."[23] Insight studies helps us develop these skills and abilities so we can work with our minds' operations more critically, effectively, and responsibly to enhance our lives and our work in school, relationships, and workplaces.

A PRACTICE-BASED APPROACH

I have spoken of Insight studies as a practice-based approach to self-knowledge and critical thinking, and over the years, Lonergan scholars have developed a variety of approaches for introducing learners to this practice-based method. In one approach, authors offer accounts that explain our minds' operations and their significance, and they invite learners to identify these operations in themselves as they read along.[24] Another provides readers with examples, often in the form of anecdotes, stories, literature, case studies, or excerpts from films.[25] The examples offer illustrations of people performing the operations in conspicuous ways. A third approach presents interesting devices like philosophical "meditations" to help draw learners into the activities of self-knowledge and critical thinking.[26] Last, authors present puzzles that engage learners directly in their own performance of the operations.[27]

The method offered here builds on the fourth of these approaches. Learners use puzzles and follow a step-by-step procedure for developing the skills of self-observation and self-understanding. I have said the approach is practice-based and I have compared the skill development path with learning to play a musical instrument. The approach is rather novel and time-consuming, so a word of explanation is in order. Why use a practice-based approach? The answer is that there are two obstacles that normally arise when we set ourselves to the task of observing and understanding our minds' operations. Gaining the relevant self-knowledge for thinking critically requires skills for overcoming these obstacles, and this requires practising exercises again and again, day after day, in much the same way we develop musical performance skills.

The first obstacle is rooted in our minds' normal orientation. Our minds are capable of doing many things, but we need to "stretch" them to do new things regularly and consistently. The moment we shift attention, they snap back to their normal orientation. Developing the skill of keeping them focused in a new way requires daily practice.

Our minds' normal inclination is to focus on the objects of consciousness: the things we see, the things we understand, the things we affirm, the courses of action we decide on and implement. To be sure, we can also notice our operations of seeing, understanding, affirming, and deciding. But investigating these operations more carefully requires stretching our minds to focus in directions they are not normally inclined to focus. Once we notice the occurrence of an operation like insight, our minds immediately snap back to their normal orientation and focus, not on the operation itself, but on the content or object of what we've understood in the insight. So, if asked about the insight, we follow our minds' normal orientation and speak about the content of what we have understood, not the operation itself. Doing anything else requires teaching our minds to stretch to keep their focus trained on the operation itself. This is quite difficult.

To overcome this obstacle, this course involves learners in the practice of solving scramble word puzzles. This puzzle type has been selected because learners are able to observe all of our operations occurring in a pattern that repeats itself over and over as each puzzle word is solved. Also, scramble word puzzles feature the most elusive of operations, the direct insight. By observing the pattern time and again, learners become familiar with the pattern and the operations. By selecting puzzles at the right level and following a precise method for puzzle solving, learners develop the skills for shifting the mind's focus away from the objects of the operations and onto the operations themselves. By doing this over and over again, learners train the mind to investigate identifiable features of the various operations, and this enables the mind to cultivate the ability to do something it previously could not have done: remain focused on the operations. This takes practice. *The method offered here involves practising the exercises thirty minutes daily, five days per week, for nine weeks.*

The second obstacle is rooted in the normal state of our minds. For most of us, most of the time, our minds are the loci of an amazing jumble of acts, images, thoughts, feelings, convictions, words, sounds, sensations, and wonderings. If called upon to stop, examine, and give an account of our minds, most of us would be at a loss to know what to say. To be sure, there are the immediate objects at the forefront of our minds. If we are in a conversation, these include our interpretation of what the other has said and what we want to say in reply. But if asked to observe and report on what's going on beyond or alongside these immediate objects, we might find it difficult to reply. This is not because there is nothing to observe but because there is simply too much to observe. We have not developed a method or skill for sorting through the various acts, events, images, feelings, words, sounds, sensations, wonderings, and convictions. Nor have we developed a method or skill for calming and focusing our minds so the cacophony settles down. These are the skills we need to learn and learning takes practice.

Overcoming the second obstacle requires learning to solve scramble word puzzles in a way that is slow, measured, and calm. Normally, when we engage with puzzles, our activities are accompanied by the dazzling cacophony of images and feelings that characterizes the bustling state of our minds. By carefully following the instructions of the modules, however, learners develop skills for quelling the mind and setting aside the feelings of frenzy or anxiety that normally accompany puzzle solving. The instructions teach learners to solve puzzles slowly rather than quickly, to focus on the doing and not the outcomes, to notice but set aside competitive and self-esteem feelings, to stop and pause time and again through the process, to disengage during the pauses, and to pause before rushing on to the next puzzle. The effect of this practice is to help learners settle their minds into a state required for observing their minds' operations. In some ways, the puzzle-solving process can be compared to some types of meditation. The practice helps create a calm, unhurried, safe, and open space for gaining the self-knowledge required for thinking critically and responsibly.

Before moving on, a brief word is in order to help clarify this distinction between our minds' operations and the content of these operations. Often, when someone is explaining something, they ask: do you have any questions? Often, we say "yes." And when we do, we focus our attention on the content of our question. But in doing so, we have also done something else. We have noticed our minds' operation of questioning. This is why we are able to answer "yes."

This second noticing – the noticing of the operation itself – is something we do frequently, but normally we do it haphazardly, without much further thought. We pursue the content of our questions, but normally we do not pursue our noticing of the operation of questioning itself. We do not investigate its features: how it feels, how it directs our attention, how it directs our action, how it is satisfied. We do not investigate our different kinds of questioning. Nor do we investigate the different roles played by questioning in understanding, verifying, valuing, and deciding. In Insight studies, the focus is on developing skills and gaining competence for making this second noticing more deliberate, more effective, and more habitual. Developing these skills takes practice. The nine learning modules offered here set you on this road of skill development in self-knowledge and critical thinking.

OUTLINE OF THE CHAPTERS AND LEARNING MODULES

The nine practice modules of the book are organized as an introductory self-knowledge and critical thinking course that can be offered either in-person or online in a variety of contexts and institutional settings. The modules do not require learners to have a prior background in any discipline, and they can be offered either independently or within the program of any discipline. The complete set can be offered as a course, or packages of the first three or first six modules can form mini-courses that can be offered alone or as components of other courses. Given that the modules are designed to build on prior modules, instructors need to follow the order of the modules so that learners begin with modules 1–3 and complete the required prior modules before starting the next.

Independent learners may choose to follow this program in a "self-help" mode. The chapters provide considerable guidance, and references to other related works are offered for learners to consult as they wish. One text that provides an excellent overview of Lonergan's work and his method of self-knowing is Patrick Byrne's *The Ethics of Discernment,* particularly chapters 1–3. I recommend these chapters as a companion text for this course. Given that challenges always arise along the learning path, especially in the first three modules, self-help learners are encouraged to contact a coach or mentor, either online or in-person, to help answer questions and provide support from time to time.[28]

There are nine learning modules in the course, and they are gathered into three groups in chapters 2, 3, and 4. Chapter 2, "Getting Started," contains modules 1–3; chapter 3, "Identifying the Operations," contains modules 4–6; chapter 4, "Feelings, Values, and Decisions," contains modules 7–9.

Chapter 2   Getting Started: Practice Modules 1–3
            Module 1: Establishing a Daily Routine of Puzzle Solving
            Module 2: A Special Procedure for Puzzle Solving
            Module 3: Focusing on Your Mind's Operations
Chapter 3   Identifying the Operations: Practice Modules 4–6
            Module 4: Differentiating Groups of Operations
            Module 5: Identifying the Operation of Direct Insight
            Module 6: Identifying the Operation of Judgment
Chapter 4   Feelings, Values, and Decisions: Practice Modules 7–9
            Module 7: Identifying Feelings and Values
            Module 8: Feelings, Values, and Decisions
            Module 9: Observing an Inner Normativity

The most important modules are the first three. Here, learners get started by finding puzzles at the right level, establishing a daily routine of puzzle solving, learning the special procedure for puzzle solving, and taking the first steps in learning to focus attention on their minds' operations. All the remaining modules build on the skills learned in the first three. So, if learners experience difficulties here, it would be wise to devote extra time to these modules to establish a good base for the remaining modules.

If instructors wish to choose one set of three modules for a stand-alone package or mini-course that provides learners with the most benefit in the shortest time, the first three modules offer the best choice. If instructors wish to make a longer course but cannot accommodate all nine modules, they can offer modules 1–6.

For instructors who are considering offering this course, it is important for you to practise the modules yourself before instructing or coaching others. At the beginning of the course, many students experience difficulties in learning how to practise the modules. As an instructor, in order to help them, you need to identify and experience these difficulties yourself. As you do, you gain insights, not only into the course material, but also into the teaching-learning process. You need to be thinking about this course as similar to teaching a musical instrument. If you have only read books and have not learned to play the instrument, you will not be very good at helping others learn to play. This is particularly important at the beginning.

If you have some background knowledge of the work of Lonergan, one approach might be to consider devoting three weeks prior to the course to learning and practising the first three modules. This would help you learn how to support students through the most difficult part of the course, "Getting Started." Then, once the course begins, you could let students know you are accompanying them as a co-learner, working alongside them, doing all the remaining practice modules of the course. This way, you could share your learning experiences with them as you move through the modules together.

The self-knowledge and critical thinking modules offered here do not require learners to have a prior background in any discipline. Insight studies can be considered a freestanding discipline. It is designed as a complement to other approaches to critical thinking; it can become an integral part of a college or university core curriculum; or it can become a core component of a program in any discipline. It can help learners of all ages in their studies, workplaces, and relationships. It is a freestanding discipline because its methods are unlike those of other disciplines like philosophy or psychology. Gaining competence in Insight studies is not primarily a matter of reading texts, constructing arguments, writing essays, writing exams, or doing social-scientific research in which learners study others. Rather, competence is gained through daily practice and skill development in the method of self-knowledge and critical thinking. It is the method for observing, investigating, and taking responsibility for the operations of our own minds.

One final note. This nine-module course is a basic introduction to Insight studies. There is a great deal more to be learned. Applying self-knowledge and critical thinking skills competently throughout life requires considerably more than can be achieved in one course.[29] What the course does offer, however, are suggestions for practising the skills that are tailored to the normal achievement levels of modules 3, 6, and 9. These suggestions are offered in the sections titled "Applying the Skills," at the end of chapters 2, 3, and 4. Also, the basic skills of this course can set learners on paths of further development that they can pursue either independently or in other courses. To provide some indication of the diverse paths of development that scholars and practitioners have pursued, chapter 5 offers six snapshots of works by authors who apply the method in diverse fields.

Scholars and practitioners in a wide range of disciplines have found the self-knowledge and critical thinking method of Lonergan to be helpful for their work.[30] Lonergan wrote many of his own works as contributions to theology. Yet the positive impacts of his achievements have not been limited to this discipline; they have been felt in many fields. The following six areas of application have been selected for the survey of chapter 5: ethics, conflict studies, sociology, psychology, philosophy, and politics. For the most part, the authors have been chosen because they focus not simply on Lonergan's ideas but on implementing the skills of self-knowledge. The texts are readable, and they offer concrete illustrations of novel insights that can be gained by learning and applying the skills that are the focus of Insight studies.

There is another reason these six authors have been chosen. It is normal for college and university disciplines to focus on students' professional and career paths. Yet the challenges that prove disruptive in workplace contexts are often not related directly to their professional training. Rather, they are often life skill challenges: relationship issues, self-esteem issues, decision-making issues, value conflicts, work-life balance issues, and issues related to the meaning and purpose of their lives. The works surveyed in chapter 5 all deal with life skill issues. They deal with ethical challenges and challenges arising in situations fraught with conflict. They deal with arguments that arise in relationships. The authors explore challenges arising when difficult problems must be solved. They deal with the "big" philosophical issues arising when we struggle with life's meaning and purpose. And they deal with troubling questions arising at the intersection between politics and religion. Insight studies offers a practice-based method for helping learners discern, understand, and take ownership of the operations of their minds. The skills of Insight studies can prove helpful in these difficult moments. The benefits of this practice-based approach to self-knowledge and critical thinking can find their way into all areas of life and work.

CHAPTER TWO

Getting Started: Practice Modules 1–3

Insight studies offers an innovative approach to self-knowledge and critical thinking, an approach that is patterned after the way we learn to play a musical instrument. It requires practising the activities of the modules daily, five days per week. Each module has a specific goal, and it is important to practise the activities regularly, even when they seem pointless or repetitive. The suggested practice time is about thirty minutes per day. Many learners come to enjoy the practice modules. Hopefully this will be your experience.

This is an introductory course and is designed for all students. In all nine modules of the course, you will be doing puzzles. As outlined in chapter 1, the goal of Insight studies is to develop the skills for noticing, understanding, verifying, and responsibly using the operations of your own mind. The puzzles are a laboratory for this learning at the introductory level. Paying attention to the operations of your own mind is not easy. But in doing puzzles one after another, your mind performs the basic operations over and over again. By following the instructions and practising regularly, you can learn to pay attention to these operations. Solving the puzzles is not the goal of the course. Rather, doing the puzzles provides the context for developing the skills required for observing and understanding your mind as it performs its operations.

In this course, you will be solving scramble word puzzles. These are also called jumble word puzzles. This puzzle type has been selected for a reason. In solving scramble words, your mind performs the operations of observing, understanding, judging, and deciding. The instructions of the modules help you develop and practise skills for noticing these operations and how they work together. By following along, step-by-step, you can learn to notice that, even when your mind seems to be jumping around, there is a pattern that emerges in which some operations build on and carry forward other operations. Scramble word puzzles offer you the opportunity to observe this pattern recur over and over again, puzzle after puzzle, day after day, week after week. Doing the modules, you become familiar with the pattern and with the distinctive features of each type of operation. Noticing this pattern takes practice, and scramble word puzzles offer a good context for practising these noticing skills.

There is another reason why scramble word puzzles have been selected. Among the various operations your mind performs, the most difficult to notice and investigate is the operation of direct insight. Direct insight is the operation in which understanding emerges. Direct insights occur suddenly and are easy to miss. Scramble word puzzles feature this operation of direct insight. When you select puzzle words that fit your own level of difficulty, you can learn to solve three or more scramble words every day using the special procedure of the modules. This means that, with daily practice, you can learn to become familiar with your direct insights. Eventually, you can learn to notice and investigate your insights when they occur, not just in the practice exercises, but in everyday life.

SELECTING PUZZLES THAT ARE RIGHT FOR YOU

Before starting the modules, it is essential that you find a source of puzzle words at the right level of difficulty for you. By this I mean that you need to have individual scramble words you can solve in a period of time between fifteen seconds and three minutes. This is something you must do for yourself, so you need to take the time required to find the right puzzle words. This is one of the most important parts of the course. If you do not find puzzle words that fit within your comfort range, the course will not work. It will be important for you to solve at least three puzzle words in every day's thirty-minute practice session, and it will be important that all of these puzzle words take you more than fifteen seconds to solve.

Start by consulting the Appendix at the back of this book. You will find lists of scramble words organized according to their number of letters. This corresponds, roughly, to levels of difficulty. Try out the scramble words and identify ones you can solve. Start with puzzle words with four letters. If you find some puzzle words in this list that take you more than fifteen seconds but less than three minutes to solve, then you have found a good starting point for yourself. If you find you cannot solve any of the puzzle words in this list within three minutes, then move over to puzzle words with three letters and start there.[1] If you find you are solving four-letter puzzle words in less than fifteen seconds, then move over to the list of words with five letters. Keep experimenting until you are able to find scramble words that you can solve in a time period between fifteen seconds and three minutes.

Once you have determined the level of difficulty that is right for you, then shop online or in a bookstore to find a "scramble word" or "jumble word" puzzle book or online source of scramble words with lots of puzzle words at this level as well as lots of puzzle words at increasingly greater levels of difficulty.[2] As you go through the modules of this course, you will likely become more proficient at solving scramble words. As you improve, you will need to move up to more difficult puzzle words in order to stay within the time range of between fifteen seconds and three minutes per puzzle word.

If you shop online, go to the online site of a bookseller and type in a search for "jumble word" or "scramble word." It would be best if you could find a number of different books that allow you to browse through some pages online. You can also do this in person at a bookstore if you wish. In bookstores, these books are often found in the books section, rather than the magazine section. Likely you will be able to find quite a few different books. A list of scramble word and jumble word book titles is provided at the end of the book.

In the modules, you will be working with the individual scramble words one at a time. Some books and online sources present the scramble words in groups of four or five along with a cartoon with a question for a "surprise answer" underneath the cartoon. If you select one of these books, you will not be working with the cartoon or the "surprise answer." The only thing you'll require is the individual puzzle words.

In the modules, you will be instructed to write each scramble word on a separate sheet of paper and to work with this sheet. This is very important. You need to set aside all books, phones, and computer devices in order to concentrate properly. The best way to do this is to sit down at a desk or table with nothing else on it but your single sheet of paper with one scramble word, and perhaps a pen or pencil and scrap paper. When the instructions refer to solving a scramble word, this means solving an individual word, not a group of scramble words or a surprise answer related to a cartoon.

In order for the Insight studies learning process to work, you will need to develop a practice routine of solving scramble words at a slow, comfortable, anxiety-free pace. This is because eventually you will need to practise developing a double-focus in your attention as you work with the scramble words. The instructions for later modules explain how to do this. Keep in mind that the goal is not getting good at puzzle solving; rather the goal is developing skills for observing and understanding the operations of your own mind.

When you first try solving scramble words, it is normal to experience anxious feelings. A good way to help alleviate these feelings is to move over to puzzle words with fewer letters that you can solve very quickly. After working with a few such words, you can move back to puzzle words with more letters. If you find that you are solving puzzle words in less than fifteen seconds, then move over to more difficult puzzle words. Keep working with more difficult scramble words until you can select ones that take you between fifteen seconds and three minutes to solve.

If you cannot solve a puzzle word in three minutes, then simply skip that word and move on to the next. If you cannot find another puzzle word on that page or in the pages nearby, then move on to other pages or books or online sources with puzzle words at your level.

If you are slow in solving puzzle words and find you can work well with words with fewer letters, this is excellent. On the other hand, if you are quick at solving puzzle words, you will encounter difficulties in these learning modules until you find puzzles that take you more than fifteen seconds to solve.

The main thing to understand is that you are not competing with others. In fact, you are not even competing with yourself. Rather, your goal is simply finding a source of puzzle words at your comfort level.

The activity of solving puzzle words provides you with a personal learning context for investigating the operations of your own mind.

If you browse through puzzle books, you may find that some books place easy puzzle words near the beginning and more difficult puzzle words towards the end. Other books, on the other hand, have both easier and more difficult puzzle words mixed together on every page. Some books have "challenger" sections with more difficult puzzle words. If your book groups puzzle words together in groups of four or five, often you will find that the groups contain some that are easy and some that are more difficult. Simply select the puzzle words that fit your level and skip over the others. Some books self-identify as offering mostly "challenger" puzzles while others may provide puzzles at all levels. Spend time looking through various available books and trying out puzzle words at various levels.

Usually you will find scramble words of varying levels of difficulty on the same page. This is normal. If you find you can solve some puzzle words and not others on that page, this is fine. Simply skip over the ones you cannot solve within the allotted time. Sometimes you will find that your anxiety level starts to rise after working with a scramble word for more than a minute. In later modules you will be provided with instructions for investigating these feelings. For now, simply notice these feelings and set them aside. Give yourself permission to simply stop working with a scramble word and move on to the next if you start getting anxious.

If English is your second or third language, or if you are not good at solving this type of word puzzle, then feel free to locate a source of scramble words with fewer letters. Do not hesitate to consult online sites or books with puzzles for children. The only thing that is important for this course is that you find puzzles that are right for you so you can solve puzzle words successfully.

Another alternative would be to use an online site that allows you to create your own scramble words. If you use such a site, you will need to work with another person and have them choose and insert words into the program. You can chat with them ahead of time about what sorts of words to insert. The "create your own" sites may also be helpful if you need a source of more difficult scramble words or words in another language.

If you find that you can work with individual scramble words for more than three minutes without anxiety feelings, this is fine. Recall, however, that you will need to solve at least three scramble words within each day's thirty-minute practice session. So, do not take too long on individual puzzle words.

MODULE 1: ESTABLISHING A DAILY ROUTINE OF PUZZLE SOLVING

You will need to find a time and place to set all other concerns and interruptions aside so you can devote your complete attention to your practice activities. You need to practise the activities alone, with no interruptions, with no cell phones, tablets, or computers within your range of attention, and with no music playing. You may keep a pen or pencil and a piece of scrap paper if you wish, but nothing else. The activities aim at achieving a state of discipline and self-mastery that is similar in some respects to some types of meditation. As you perform the activities over and over each week, your goal will be to practise solving your scramble words at a slow, measured pace, achieving a state of relative emotional calm, a calm that retains the anticipation and energy of enquiry but is freed from other performance-related anxieties that often accompany puzzle-type activities.

> **MODULE 1: ESTABLISHING A DAILY ROUTINE OF PUZZLE SOLVING**
>
> Now that you have located a source of puzzle words that are right for you, the task of this first module is simply to practise solving puzzle words. The recommended practice time is thirty minutes daily.
>
> **Goals of This Module**
>
> - To gain a basic familiarity with solving scramble words
> - To practise solving individual scramble words in a time period between fifteen seconds and three minutes
> - To solve at least three scramble words in each day's practice session

- To begin developing an ability to solve scramble words at a slow, measured pace with a calm, anxiety-free mind

Instructions: Important!
Make sure you do your puzzle-solving in a room by yourself, in a quiet place, with no other persons present.

Make sure you have no computers, cell phones, or music playing nearby, and make sure you have no interruptions.

Make sure you do not impose any competitive expectations on yourself, simply settle into a pace that allows you to solve puzzle words slowly and calmly.

Prepare each day's session by selecting a list of ten puzzle words within your estimated comfort range and write each puzzle word on a separate sheet of paper so you end up with ten individual sheets of paper. Work with one sheet at a time and place all the other sheets off your table or desk, out of your field of vision and concentration. You may bring a pencil or pen and a sheet of scrap paper if you wish.

If you are struggling to solve scramble words, here are some tricks and strategies you may find helpful:

1. On any page of scramble words, you are likely to find some puzzle words that are easier and some that are more difficult. Start by selecting words of fewer letters. Then, skip to other pages and only do the puzzle words with the fewer letters. Do not feel that you must solve all the puzzle words on any one page.
2. Scramble words are constructed to confuse you, and one way they do this is by changing the sound or rhythm of the word. So, if the scramble word seems like one syllable, try rearranging the letters so it sounds like two syllables. If the vowels are separated, try combining them in a typical pattern that is different from the one presented. If there is an "s," try putting it in a different place, such as at the end of the word.

3 One way of starting is often to simply write out a completely different arrangement of the letters and work with this. Pronouncing the word out loud often provides auditory clues that the printed scramble word does not provide.

When starting out, learners may experience some anxious feelings. This is normal. Try your best to notice your anxious feelings, acknowledge them, and then set them aside.

If you are working with puzzle words that are too difficult, your anxiety will get in the way of your learning. If so, move over to puzzle words with fewer letters so you can solve your scramble words within the time period.

Keep on hand a source of easy scramble words that you can solve in less than fifteen seconds. If you start getting anxious, you will find that shifting over to one of these provides you with a boost of self-confidence that eases anxious feelings. Then, move back to solving puzzle words at the more difficult level once you've restored your confidence.

If you find you solve a scramble word in less than fifteen seconds, simply move on to the next. It is normal to find some puzzle words easier and others more difficult. If you are able to solve each puzzle word in less than fifteen seconds, move up to more difficult puzzle words with more letters.

MODULE 2: A SPECIAL PROCEDURE FOR PUZZLE SOLVING

After the first module devoted to practising solving scramble words, this module introduces a specific procedure for solving puzzle words. The procedure involves dividing the process into three stages and learning to engage, pause and disengage, then re-engage in the solving process. In total, you will pause four times: immediately after the first stage; part way through the second stage; at the end of the second stage; and at the end of the third stage.

The procedure is designed to prepare you for learning a new skill in module 3, the skill of dividing your attention to focus on your mind's operations. To do this, you need to achieve a state of discipline and self-mastery that is similar in some respects to some types of meditation. As you perform the activities of this procedure over and over, you learn to pause at four specific times during the procedure in order to provide "spaces" in the process when your mind disengages from focusing on puzzle solving.

As in the previous module, it is important that you find a time and place to set all other concerns and interruptions aside so you can devote your complete attention to the activities. It is best to practise the activities alone, with no interruptions, with no cell phones, tablets, or computers within your range of attention.

Throughout the process, you may observe various types of feelings arising: feelings related to performance anxiety, self-esteem, competitive pressure, or sheer determination. Some of these feelings may be positive in the sense that they help you solve your scramble words. But the positive feelings can also get in the way if left uncontrolled. Focusing on success can distract you from the real business of this course: learning to focus your attention on your mind's operations. On the other hand, some of these feelings may be negative in the sense that you may feel you'll never get it, or you'll be humiliated, or you want to give up and withdraw. You may observe yourself developing justifications related to these feelings. You may observe yourself oscillating between these two sets of positive and negative feelings.

Your goal is to achieve some measure of mastery over these feelings, to harness them so they work for you. These feelings are your friends, so do not think badly of them. They help protect and develop you. But, in a process like this, if left uncontrolled, they can place barriers that block your learning. So, when you set them aside, think of this as helping tame them so they work for you instead of against you. You will not get rid of the feelings. Nor should you. In a later module, you will focus on these feelings, observing and examining them. For now, simply notice the feelings and set them aside. Give yourself permission to solve each puzzle slowly.

MODULE 2: A SPECIAL PROCEDURE FOR PUZZLE SOLVING

Goals of This Module

- To practise a method for solving scramble words in which you divide the process into three stages
- To learn to engage, pause and disengage, then re-engage in the solving process
- In total, you will pause four times: immediately after the first stage, part way through the second stage, at the end of the second stage, and at the end of the third stage

Write each individual scramble word on a single sheet of paper and put the puzzle book aside, away from your field of attention. Prior to each day's practice session, prepare a stack of ten sheets of paper with one puzzle word on each sheet. If you find you are encountering quite a few scramble words that are either too easy or too hard, prepare more sheets so you can easily skip to the next puzzle word. Each sheet should have nothing else on it but the one puzzle word. You may also have a pen or pencil and a piece of scrap paper with you.

Instructions: Three Stages

1 Stage 1: In the first stage (the shortest stage), observe the puzzle word, then immediately pause and disengage. Sit quietly for ten to fifteen seconds, refraining from engaging in puzzle solving. It is important to practise the skill of sitting anxiety-free in this state of non-engagement. Work at emptying your mind rather than simply shifting your focus onto something else. At first, your mind will pull you towards engaging with the puzzle word. Notice this pull but resist it. Aim for a relatively calm, anxiety-free state. This is not easy to do. After ten to fifteen seconds, move on to the second stage and re-engage in puzzle solving.

2 Stage 2: In the second stage (the longest stage), engage in trying to solve the puzzle word for about ten to fifteen seconds but stop and disengage before hitting on a solution. As in the first stage, pause and sit for ten to fifteen seconds, working to achieve a calm, anxiety-free state as you did during the pause of the first stage. I find that putting my eyes out of focus helps keep my mind free from focusing on the puzzle word or on something else. After the pause, go back into stage 2 and re-engage in solving your scramble word.

While engaged in solving, work at achieving a relatively calm, controlled pace of solving puzzle words, unencumbered by performance-related, competitive, or self-esteem anxieties. While puzzles are usually presented as requiring you to achieve solutions quickly, this is not the goal in this procedure. Quite the opposite.

In the second stage, you will eventually hit on a possible solution to the puzzle word. Immediately when this occurs, pause again and disengage, sitting quietly and calmly for ten to fifteen seconds. After the pause, re-engage with your scramble word.

Notice that, in stage 2, you pause and disengage twice. You may find that you wish to practise pausing and disengaging more frequently during stage 2. If so, insert your additional pauses before you hit on a solution.

3 Stage 3: In the third stage (the final stage), you will find yourself working with your solution, reflecting on it, examining it, asking about it, and doing things with it. This may take you very little time, or it may take you a bit longer. You may end up rejecting your proposed solution. If so, you will go back to stage 2. Eventually you will arrive at some sort of closure to the process. Once you conclude with the puzzle word, pause and disengage, sitting quietly again for ten to fifteen seconds. Then, move on to the next puzzle word.

It is important to practise remaining calm and anxiety-free for ten to fifteen seconds after you finish each puzzle word. You will likely notice that you need to battle the desire to move on. Notice this and set it aside.

Things That Don't Matter
It does not matter how long the complete process takes you for each scramble word as long as you manage to complete this procedure successfully at least three times during each day's practice session and as long as each puzzle takes at least fifteen seconds to solve. Of course, solving puzzles is never completely within your control. So, sometimes you will take longer with one or another puzzle word and will not complete three successfully within your thirty-minute practice period. If so, feel free either to take longer or to rest comfortable with the puzzle words you've solved. On other occasions, you will complete your three scramble words successfully in less than thirty minutes. If so, feel free either to quit early or to do more puzzle words.

It does not matter whether you end up skipping a lot of scramble words because you are solving them too quickly, or because you find you cannot solve them at all. If so, in each case simply move on to the next one. The important thing is that, in any day's session, you keep an eye on the time with the aim of completing the procedure successfully for at least three scramble words.

It does not matter whether you are doing easy or difficult puzzles. Make sure you have access to puzzle words that are both easier and more difficult, so you can continually adjust your puzzles to fit your comfort level. If you are feeling bad or anxious about your abilities, notice these feelings but set them aside. Being slow will not hamper your ability to succeed with this activity. In fact, it can work to your advantage. Your challenge will be mastering your negative performance anxiety feelings. Work at this by

> following the steps, giving yourself permission to solve only the occasional puzzle word, and skipping over the others. Take the time to sit calmly in the midst of the process.

EXCURSUS: INTRODUCING SELF-KNOWING

To this point, you have been working to find a source of scramble word puzzles at your own comfort level, you have been practising solving them, and you have been practising the special procedure of module 2. Likely you have noticed that the procedure seems a bit odd. It invites you to engage in puzzle solving in a way that is different from the way you naturally tackle puzzles.

Normally, you feel the urge to work quickly, and you feel some sort of competition, either with yourself or with others. You feel like you are expected to solve puzzles that are more and more difficult, and to solve them more and more quickly. This procedure, on the other hand, requires that you resist all of these feelings. In fact, you have to go against them: to choose puzzles that are less difficult rather than more so; to deliberately slow down; to practise engaging, then pausing and disengaging; and to pause quietly at the end before rushing on to the next.

The goal of this short excursus is to give you a bit of background on Insight studies in order to explain why you need to learn to practise the puzzles this way.

To begin, let me introduce the term "self-appropriation."[3] It is the term that the philosopher Bernard Lonergan developed to refer to the learning approach that is used in this Insight studies course. In this course, we use the terms "self-knowledge" and "self-knowing" to speak about self-appropriation. Lonergan's theory of knowing explains the operations of the mind. What is distinctive in his approach is the way we learn about our minds' operations.

So let me illustrate what I mean by the expressions "operations of the mind" and "the way we learn about our minds' operations." I will do this by referring to your experiences practising the modules during the past couple weeks.

In each puzzle that you solved successfully, something happened to you. I will use the term, "direct insight," to name this event. Likely by now, after practising the procedure, you have discovered that the procedure invites you to pause immediately after this event happens. And likely you have discovered that pausing at this moment can be rather difficult. You have to practise doing the pause over and over again in order to stop your mind from rushing onto something else.

You may have been asking: why do I need to learn to pause at this moment?

Here is a preliminary answer. Your mind has the ability to do two things at once. But normally your mind is inclined to focus on one of these and not the other. Your mind has a normal appetite or inclination that you need to resist in order to learn to focus attention on the second thing. Pausing at this moment interrupts this normal inclination. It makes space for investigating the second thing. The pause gives you the space to begin learning to focus your attention towards the second thing.

So then, what are these two things?

The first of these things is focusing on what I will call "the object of consciousness." So, for example, when I wonder about a tree, my mind focuses on the tree as it is present to me as an object of questioning or enquiry. When I examine the twigs and get the insight that the tree is an ash tree, my mind focuses on the tree as an object of understanding. But all the while, as I engage in these activities, in the background, my mind is also doing a second thing. It is making present to me the operations of observing, questioning, and understanding. This is why I can notice them. So, for example, when I'm deep in thought questioning something, if I'm asked by someone what I'm doing, I'm able to tell them: "I'm wondering." If I get an insight and shout out "Aha!" and someone asks what happened, I'm able to tell them: "I just got an insight!" This is because my mind, in addition to doing the first thing, is also able to do the second thing.

I am able to make these statements to the other person because I'm able to notice the operations of questioning and insight in myself. And I can notice them because my mind is always doing two things at once: performing the operations, plus making the operations present to me as they are performed. In fact, it is quite appropriate to say that this second thing, making the operations present to me, provides me with a second field of data that I can investigate more deliberately as I learn the required skills. Lonergan calls this second field of data, "the data of consciousness."

When I say that my mind is doing two things at once, I am not saying I can easily pay attention to both things. In fact, this is a difficult skill that must be learned. Paying explicit attention to the operations themselves (the observing, the questioning, the direct insights, and the verifying) takes a lot of practice. It is like learning to play the violin. It is definitely doable. But it requires the long, hard road of skill development. It is difficult because it goes against my mind's normal inclination. It has to be learned, not by trying to do two things simultaneously, but by practising deliberately to shift attention back and forth between the two things.

Interestingly, Lonergan notes that the disciplined study of this second field of data, the data of my mind's operations, can be called "empirical," even though it does not involve focusing exclusively on the data of the senses. To be sure, this is an odd way of using the term, "empirical." But it does highlight the fact that the data of consciousness can indeed be investigated, understood, and verified with greater control and precision when we acquire the relevant skills.

So, to summarize, the operations that your mind performs are indeed operations that are present to you in everyday life, and it is not difficult to notice them from time to time. It is not difficult to find a great deal of evidence in support of this. But it is one thing to notice something occasionally, it is something entirely different to cultivate the skill of noticing and investigating it consistently and accurately. This is the skill that has to be learned. This is what you begin learning in the next module.

It is not easy to learn how to shift your mind's attention away from the direction of its normal inclination. But it is possible. And when you follow up on this possibility, you gain control of your mind in a totally new way. The upshot is a new way of exercising responsibility as a person and citizen. Mastering this skill is a good way of taking possession of yourself by taking control of your mind.

The new direction is a skill that has to be learned. And, like any new skill (e.g., driving a car, learning to ski, learning to use a new computer program, playing the violin), at first you find it almost impossible. Then, with some practice you can do it, but it is difficult. Then, with more practice, you can do it better, but you are still a bit awkward and clumsy. Then, as you get better, you eventually learn to do it rather smoothly, rather well.

So, this is what you are starting to do in this module, learning a new skill. The skill is learning to shift your mind's attention away from the objects of consciousness and towards focusing on your mind's operations. The skill requires learning to engage your mind deliberately in investigating the operations it performs in everyday living, the operations of experiencing, understanding, verifying, and deciding.

MODULE 3: FOCUSING ON YOUR MIND'S OPERATIONS

In light of this short explanation, the goal of module 2 was to begin learning to control your engagement in the solving process so that you open up pauses for attending explicitly to the operation you have just performed. This week's module introduces what you will be doing during these pauses. In the first pause, you create a space so that you can pay attention to the difference between merely seeing something and engaging in questioning what you are seeing. In the midst of the questioning process, the space created by the second pause invites you to focus your attention on your state of consciousness while questioning but before understanding. In the third pause, the space created by the pause invites you to focus on the transformation that happens with the insight. This allows you to observe what happens to you as you shift from "before-the-insight" to "after-the-insight." In the fourth pause, the space created by the pause allows you to focus on the verification operation that arises after you get the insight.

> **MODULE 3: FOCUSING ON YOUR MIND'S OPERATIONS**
> After locating a source of puzzles, practising solving scramble words, and practising the special procedure of module 2, this module invites you to begin learning to focus

your attention on your mind's operations as you solve your puzzle words.

Goals of This Module

- To begin developing the skill of shifting attention back and forth between the objects of consciousness and the operations your mind performs as you solve scramble words
- To begin taking notes on your observations and writing a one-paragraph report at the end of the week

Preparation

For each day's activity, prepare your stack of ten sheets of paper with one puzzle word on each sheet, as in previous modules. Make sure you set all other concerns and interruptions aside and practise the activities alone, with no cell phones, tablets, or computers.

This week you will also need a second sheet of paper each day for recording your observations. Prepare your sheet of paper with the title: "What My Mind Is Doing" and the date at the top.

Instructions

Your task is to work at solving your scramble words using the procedure of module 2 and to record your observations on "What My Mind Is Doing" in each of the four pauses in the solving process.

During each of the four pauses, observe what your mind was doing just prior to the pause. In making your observations, follow these instructions and ask yourself the following questions:

1 First Pause. During the first pause, immediately after reading the scramble word and before engaging in solving, notice how your mind "urges" you towards solving, and notice how difficult it is to resist this urge

to engage. Ask yourself: what can I observe about the difference between (a) merely seeing the scramble word and (b) engaging in the solving? Likely you are having trouble holding back your mind from engaging in solving. What can you observe about your mind's urge to engage? Look at something else in the room and notice that simply "seeing" this other thing is a remarkably different experience from "seeing" the scramble word. Write down any observations you can formulate on "What My Mind Is Doing" in response to these instructions and questions.

2 Second Pause. After engaging with the puzzle word but before hitting on a possible solution, notice the tension you are experiencing. Ask yourself: what can I observe about the tension I am feeling between what my mind wants to achieve and what it has not yet achieved? Likely you are finding yourself dynamized by the solving process, and this dynamism carries you in a very particular direction. But notice that there is a strange feature to this direction: you do not know the destination! What can you observe about this "going somewhere," whose central feature is that you do not know where you are going? Write down any observations you can formulate on "What My Mind Is Doing" in response to these instructions and questions.

3 Third Pause. Immediately after you hit on a possible solution, record your observations on what has just happened to you. Ask yourself: what can I observe about the difference between my state of mind before the insight and my state of mind after the insight? Notice that some sort of transformation has just occurred in you. What features can you observe about this transformation? What can you observe about the difference between the "before" and "after" states? Write down any observations you can formulate on "What My

Mind Is Doing" in response to these instructions and questions.

4 Fourth Pause. After you have reflected on your solution, examined it, done something further, then finished with the scramble word, notice what your mind was doing during this final stage. Ask yourself: what can I observe about the operations my mind performs between getting an insight and finally resting satisfied with it? Likely you are observing some questions arising after you get an insight. How are these questions different from the questions that dynamize you before getting the insight? What can you observe about the operations your mind performs in order to be satisfied that an insight is acceptable? Write down any observations you can formulate on "What My Mind Is Doing" in response to these instructions and questions.

5 Final Report. After the week's five practice sessions, you will have five sheets of paper with notes on your observations. Read over your observations, think about them, and then write a one-paragraph summary of what you have learned from your practice sessions. In your report, focus on your progress in achieving the goals of this week's activity rather than on the positive or negative feelings related to performance anxiety, self-esteem, or competitive pressure.

Your observations in this module are only a beginning. They need not be long. As you go through future modules, you will have many more opportunities to explore your mind's operations in greater depth. Also, as you practise the modules, you will get better at making observations during each of the four pauses.

One of the difficulties you will experience will be distinguishing between your mind's operations and the content of the puzzle. Your mind's natural orientation is to direct your attention towards the content of the puzzle. In this module, you begin practising the skill of resisting this natural orientation in order to focus on the operations. One way of doing this is to focus on differences. Notice the words "difference" and "different" in the instructions and focus on them.

In making notes, try to describe the various operations by using words or short descriptor phrases. In order to keep your attention focused on the operations rather than the content of the puzzles, use action verbs that point to the "doing" rather than nouns that point to the "content" of the puzzle. To use an analogy, think about the sentence: "I write a letter." The verb "write" points to the action I am performing whereas the noun "letter" points to the content of "what" I am writing.

As with last week's activity, you will observe positive or negative feelings related to performance anxiety, self-esteem, or competitive pressure. Again, observe these feelings, but set them aside and focus on what your mind is doing immediately prior to each of the four pauses in the process.

Gaining competency in the skills involved in this week's module will take much longer than a week of practice sessions. So, remain content with beginnings. Think of this week as similar to your third week in a lifelong program of learning to play the violin.

APPLYING THE SKILLS

The goal of Insight studies is to assist you in developing skills that can prove helpful in school, relationships, and workplaces. At this point in the process, after module 3, you are still near the beginning. Yet there are skills you are learning that you can practise applying in everyday life.

In module 3, you began practising the skill of shifting attention to focus on the operations your mind performs as you solve scramble words. You may have found that the most dramatic operation in the process is the operation of direct insight, the operation in which you "get it!" Yet you may also have found this to be an elusive operation, a difficult operation to observe. Much easier to observe is the operation of questioning. This is the operation you notice during the first pause. It is the operation that "urges" you towards solving, the operation that can be difficult to resist. It is the operation that provides the "tension" you experience during the solving process before the second pause, the tension that dynamizes you in the direction towards a solution. The operation of questioning arises again after the third pause, when your mind shifts to reflect on your insight.

The operation of questioning is an easier operation to notice in everyday life because it has a duration. It is not fleeting, nor does it disappear quickly to give way to other operations. It can occupy your mind for long periods of time. Given this, a good way to begin applying the skills is to practise noticing your operations of questioning. Questioning is one of the most valuable resources you have at your disposal for dealing with life's complexities. Noticing your questioning is the first step towards becoming more deliberate and capable in mobilizing this resource on your behalf.

One of the first places you can notice your own questioning is in conversations.[4] When another person is speaking to you, if you are a good listener, your mind's focus is on figuring out the meaning of what they are saying. A good place to begin is to think of the conversation as a puzzle like your scramble word puzzle. While they are speaking, your mind spontaneously engages in the operation of questioning: what is the meaning they are trying to express? Sometimes an answer arises quickly. But still, you wonder whether your answer is correct. Have you misunderstood them? You wonder about words or expressions you have not understood. You wonder whether there are things you have missed. All of these involve the operation of questioning. Stop and notice your mind performing this operation.

Doing this in the middle of a conversation may distract you from the topic of the conversation. And, initially, your conversation partner may find this annoying. But if you take the time to explain what you are doing, they may feel appreciated. You can explain that you are working at developing your conversation skills. What greater gesture of respect can you offer them than your genuine curiosity?

Another way to notice questioning in conversations is to notice when it is absent. Sometimes you jump to conclusions.[5] Sometimes you feel threatened by them, and your mind closes down or constricts.[6] Sometimes you are certain of your own position and refuse to wonder about theirs. On these occasions, notice that you can deliberately pause and open the doors of your mind to permit your curiosity and questioning to emerge. Try doing this. Try it first in simple situations, and then in more emotionally charged situations. Notice what happens to you when you do this. Notice what happens to the conversation when you do this.

As your skills develop, so too will you observe a development in your ability to apply the skills, both in the learning modules and in everyday life. Something else often accompanies skill development, and this is the ability to envision new directions in your appetite for development. Sometimes this breeds its own impatience and frustration. You begin envisioning new things you would like to accomplish, and you get impatient with the pace of the process. This may be frustrating, but it is certainly normal. Like playing the violin, there is no "quick fix." As in all life adventures, you are invited to enjoy and appreciate the journey as well as the destination.

CHAPTER THREE

Identifying the Operations: Practice Modules 4–6

In the three modules of chapter 2, you were introduced to a novel approach to self-knowledge and critical thinking. Rather than reading books, listening to lectures, or writing essays, you spent approximately thirty minutes daily practising activities and exercises in much the same way you would practise learning a musical instrument. The aim of the course is to help you develop the skills required for observing, understanding, and responsibly using the operations of your own mind. After three modules devoted to "Getting Started," the three modules of this chapter build on these to help develop skills for identifying two of your mind's most important operations: direct insight and judgment.

As in the prior chapter, the modules of this chapter engage you in solving scramble word puzzles and making observations on the operations your mind performs in this process. In order to learn the self-observation skills, you need to solve the puzzles. But the goal is not solving puzzles. Rather, puzzle solving provides the context or laboratory for learning how to make observations on your mind's operations. This learning is not "acquiring information." Rather, it is a form of skill development learning. Paying attention to your mind's operations requires considerable skill development. It is not easy. But it can be learned with practice. The modules show you how to practise.

After three weeks of practice, you have likely observed that your mind is a locus of considerable activity. There are a lot of diverse things going on. In addition to the operations of puzzle solving, your mind also presents you with flows of images, feelings, faces, frowns, sounds, questions, and arguments. Many of these affect your confidence or self-esteem. Perhaps you have a flow of background chatter that is fairly constant. You may have music "playing" in your mind. When you engage with a scramble word and focus your attention, you may start exercising some control over these operations and background events. Still, this control is seldom complete.

Even if you have been able to block out some of your mind's background "noise" and set aside some of the challenges to self-esteem, you have likely noticed that your mind is still bouncing around from one operation to another. Your mind does not walk forward methodically step-by-step. Rather, it jumps around from one activity to another and from one image to another. It tries out this, then that, and flips back and forth among a variety of activities, images, possibilities, questions, and lines of approach.

Given this, your first thought might be that your mind lacks order or method. If this were true, however, you would not be able to solve puzzles with any regularity. To be sure, your mind does a lot of jumping around. But in the midst of the jumping around, a self-organizing structure can be observed emerging. The modules of this chapter help you develop the skills for noticing and focusing attention on this self-organizing structure. In module 4 you begin by "Differentiating Groups of Operations." Module 5 helps you develop skills required for "Identifying the Operation of Direct Insight." And module 6 helps you develop skills required for "Identifying the Operation of Judgment."

MODULE 4: DIFFERENTIATING GROUPS OF OPERATIONS

In module 2 you practised a special procedure for puzzle solving, and in module 3 you began developing the skill of shifting attention back and forth between the objects of consciousness and the operations your mind performs as you solve scramble words. This module builds on the prior weeks' skills by focusing on how your mind groups diverse operations towards two specific goals. In particular, you will be focusing on two groups of operations: (1) the operations that culminate in the direct insight that achieves the goal of understanding; and (2) the operations that culminate in the judgment that achieves the goal of verification. This week's activity also involves writing down your daily observations, and at week's end, preparing a one-paragraph report and drawing a simple diagram of the stages and pauses in the solving process.

For each day's activity, prepare your sheets of paper with your scramble words in the same way you have done for previous modules. Make sure you set all other concerns and interruptions aside and practise the activities alone, with no cell phones, tablets, or computers within attention range.

This week you will also need an additional worksheet each day for recording your observations. Prepare your worksheet with the title "What My Mind Is Doing," as well as the module number and the date at the top.

MODULE 4: DIFFERENTIATING GROUPS OF OPERATIONS

Your task this week is to work at solving the scramble words, and in the pauses, observe what your mind is doing, as well as how it groups operations towards the two specific goals of understanding and verification.

Goals of This Module

- To practise observing how your mind groups operations towards the two specific goals of understanding and verification
- To draw a simple diagram illustrating the three stages in the solving process and the location of the four pauses
- To take notes on your observations and write a one-paragraph report at the end of the week on what you have learned

As in prior modules, your observing will tend to focus on the content of the scramble words. Try to set this aside and focus on the operations and groups of operations that your mind is performing.

Again, as in prior modules, you will observe positive or negative feelings related to performance anxiety, self-esteem, or competitive pressure. Observe these feelings but set them aside and focus on what your mind is doing through the process.

Instructions
During each pause, observe what your mind was doing immediately prior to the pause. Make a mental note of your observations so you can record them on your worksheet after you finish each scramble word. The following questions are offered as guides to help make your observations:

1 In the first stage during the first pause, ask yourself: why is it so difficult to hold my mind back from engaging in solving? When you disengage, you are attempting to hold yourself in the operation of simply experiencing – in this case, simply seeing the letters. But remaining in this operation of simply experiencing requires holding your mind back from another operation. Notice the tug and pull of this other operation, and notice how it wants to carry you into stage 2 towards a goal.
2 In the second stage during the second pause, after engaging with the scramble word for a short while but before finding a solution, notice that your mind performs a variety of diverse operations. Make a mental note of some of these diverse operations. Then, notice how these various operations are coordinated by one particular operation. This coordinating operation is the questioning. Notice that, in stage 2, this is a specific type of questioning with a specific type of goal. What is this goal? Notice how the operation of questioning pulls you, dynamizes you, and energizes you by orienting you towards this goal. Notice how the questioning can orient you towards

its goal even when it does not know what the goal is. Notice how strange this is.

3   In the second stage during the third pause, immediately after gaining a direct insight, but before moving on to the next stage, notice that you are now in a different state than before the insight. What can you observe about this change of state? Notice how strange this is. What happens to your questioning once you gain the direct insight? What happens to you? Notice the relationship between the questioning and this new state that arises in you when the insight occurs. Notice how all the other operations you have performed in stage 2 are grouped together and coordinated in service of the goal that is present to you now in this new state.

4   In the third stage during the fourth pause, after you have examined your solution and finished with it, notice that your mind, again, has performed a variety of diverse operations. Make note of some of these operations. Then notice how these operations are grouped together and coordinated by the questioning. Notice the difference between this questioning and the questioning in stage 2. How would you describe this difference? Notice how, finally, these operations come to an end, and your mind moves into a state of relative rest. The operation that finishes the process is the judgment. As in the prior stage, notice how all the operations you have performed in stage 3 are grouped together and coordinated in service of the goal.

After the week's practice sessions, read over your notes and draw a simple diagram illustrating how the various operations are grouped into three stages. Label the various components in the diagram. Insert the location of the four pauses in your diagram. Think about the amount of time spent in each stage. Can you capture these time durations in your diagram?

> After the week's sessions, read over your notes and write a one-paragraph summary of what you have learned from your practice sessions. In your report, focus on your progress in achieving the goals of this week's module rather than the positive or negative feelings related to performance anxiety, self-esteem, or competitive pressure.

Gaining competency in the skills required for this week's activity will take more than a week or two of practice sessions. So, do not worry if you feel like you are only beginning. These practice sessions are meant to be introductory. They provide a basis for further modules that build on them. You will have lots of opportunities to continue practising these skills in future modules.

EXCURSUS: SOME OBSERVATIONS ON THE SKILL DEVELOPMENT PROCESS

As noted, this course offers a novel approach to self-knowledge and critical thinking, an approach that is more like learning a musical instrument than like learning philosophy or history. The aim is to help you develop the skills required for observing, understanding, and responsibly using the operations of your own mind. If you practise these skills, they can help you in other studies. At this point, I would like to pause and offer some observations on the skill development process. For some of you, the process may be going well. For others, however, things may not be going so well. You may need to go back to clear some hurdles that will be important if you wish to continue.

Skill development is an unsettling affair. At first, when you try something new, you are not able to do it very well. Sometimes you cannot do it at all. You only learn by doing, so you need to try again and again. Challenges to self-esteem are always getting in the way. Eventually, you stumble on the basics, and this provides you with something to practise over and over again. By carefully following the instructions step-by-step, you build up your skills layer by layer. At every step along the way, you need to navigate the challenges and blockages presented by feelings of frustration, performance anxiety, or competitive frenzy.

To this point in the skill development process, you have had to navigate three significant hurdles. The first and most important has been finding a supply of puzzle words at your right level. Without this, you cannot even begin. You cannot practise any of the modules. If you think you have been practising the modules but have not been solving puzzle words, then you have been mistaken: you have not yet begun. If perchance you are still struggling with this, you need to go back to the beginning and spend time trying out puzzle words with fewer letters. There is no shame in this. You simply need to identify scramble words you can solve within a time period of between fifteen seconds and three minutes. You need to find a book or online source that provides you with an ample supply of scramble words within this difficulty range. Only you can do this. And once you do, you're ready.

The second hurdle has been learning to notice and set aside your feelings of competitive frenzy or performance anxiety. If your puzzle solving is constantly being derailed by either one, you cannot focus on learning the self-observation skills of the modules. To be sure, you will never get rid of these feelings completely. But you need to be able to set them aside enough to allow you to focus your mind on both puzzle solving and learning the self-observation skills.

The third hurdle has been learning to shift your focus of attention back and forth between your objects of consciousness and your mind's operations. The mind normally directs your attention to your objects of consciousness: the things you experience, understand, verify, and decide to do. But all the while, your mind is also performing the operations of experiencing, understanding, verifying, and deciding. These, too, are present to you. But they are more difficult to notice with any regularity. Because they are present to your mind, you do notice them occasionally. Still, there is a big difference between noticing them occasionally and observing them regularly. Observing, understanding, and responsibly using your mind's operations regularly require considerable skill development. A major step in this development is learning to shift your focus of attention back and forth between your objects of consciousness and your mind's operations.

Clearing the three hurdles brought you to module 4, where you began "Differentiating Groups of Operations." Once you achieve some success in focusing attention on your operations of consciousness, you find yourself in a "zone" that is teeming with diverse activities. You begin noticing that your mind is the locus of a flow of diverse images, thoughts, feelings, questions, conversations, sounds, and faces. Once you engage in puzzle solving following the instructions of module 4, you begin differentiating the operations into groups that are characterized by their objects or goals. For the purpose of this introductory course, we now focus on two of the most important of these operations: the direct insight and the judgment.

EXCURSUS: INTRODUCING THE THEORY OF KNOWING

Before moving on to module 5, this excursus offers some information that may help respond to questions you might have. It may appear somewhat complex and is not essential for you at this stage in the course. Yet you may find it interesting. I offer this information to help provide some background and clear up some possible confusion that might arise for learners who have read texts on the work of Lonergan. My effort in this excursus is to make connections between the work you are doing in the modules and the theory of knowing presented in these texts.[1]

You have been working with a procedure for solving scramble words, the procedure of module 2. The procedure invites you to practise pausing and disengaging at specific moments in the process. You may have wondered why the pauses are placed at these particular moments. Also, you may have wondered why the instructions of the modules invite you to focus on some observations and not others.

The first pause is located at the very beginning of the solving process in order to help you observe the difference between merely seeing the scramble word and engaging with it. When your mind engages with it, you are no longer merely seeing. You are seeing plus doing something else, mostly questioning. Most of the time, when we see a word, we do not merely see it: we also understand a meaning. With a scramble word, however, we cannot understand it until we solve the puzzle. This provides a laboratory for noticing the difference between the operation of merely seeing and the operations involved in questioning for understanding.

In this theory of knowing, the various sensory operations like seeing and hearing are gathered into a group called "experiencing." And we differentiate these from the operations of the second group called "understanding." The term "experience" has a specific technical meaning and is frequently misunderstood as this philosophical usage does not carry some of the normal meanings of ordinary language. Another expression whose meaning is closer to this would be "observing data." In the sciences, there is a clear difference between observing and describing data accurately, on the one hand, and the various operations that are performed in service of understanding and explaining these data, on the other. In this approach, the term "experience" is closer to the expression "observing data" as it is used in the sciences. The first pause is located right at the beginning in order to help you notice this difference.

Once you engage in solving, your mind launches into a host of operations other than seeing, and here the guiding operation is questioning. Of course, you continue seeing. But along with seeing, your mind also performs the operations of the second group, the group whose objective is "understanding." The second pause is located in the middle of this second group, and it is located there so you can observe some of these operations. What is important, however, is not getting a list of these various operations, but identifying the operation whose emergence achieves the goal of this second group, the direct insight. The third pause is located immediately after this operation of direct insight. With the direct insight, what emerges is understanding, and what we understand is a possible solution to the puzzle.

The word "possible" is important. This is because there is a difference between mere understanding and verified understanding. After the third pause, your mind shifts from the operations that aim at understanding into a new group of operations, the operations that head towards "judgment." These are the operations of verification. Verification involves a new type of questioning, a questioning that reflects on the insight and asks if it has the right features for you to judge it to be correct. In scramble words, you will notice that you count the letters and check to determine whether all the letters are accounted for. These are your questions for verification. When you can answer "yes" to all the questions, then your mind makes the judgment that your insight is correct. With the achievement of verification, your mind is finished with this puzzle.

This theory of knowing offers an explanation of the three groups of operations that your mind uses in puzzle solving. It is the threefold structure of experience, understanding, and judgment. The pauses in the modules are located where they are in order to help direct attention to specific observations that can help you differentiate these three groups of operations in your daily practice.

If you have been reading other works on Lonergan's philosophy, you have likely encountered authors speaking about a fourfold structure of "experience, understanding, judgment, and decision."[2] In this list, there are four groups of operations, not three. Also, scholars working on applications of Insight Theory to fields like conflict may speak about a "double loop" of operations.[3] In the double loop diagram, depending on the version presented, you may find six or more different types of operations listed, not three. How are we to make sense of these differences?

Scholars recognize that in earlier works, Lonergan refers to a three-fold structure of experience, understanding, and judgment. Then, midway in his career, he shifts to speaking about a fourfold structure that adds the operation of "decision" to this list. One of the prevailing interpretations explains this shift by pointing out that the fourth term, "decision," does not simply add another operation to the previous three. Rather, when our minds move into the mode of decision and action, we re-engage all the prior operations in a new way towards a new set of goals, the goals of value and action.[4] Scholars explain this reactivation of the prior three by appealing to the image of a second loop of operations.

This means that the mind mobilizes the operations of understanding and judgment in two different ways: the first to focus on questions about fact (What is it? Is it so?), and the second to focus on questions about value and action (What to do? Is this the right thing to do?). The final operation – decision – marks the culmination and implementation of the operations of understanding and judgment when they investigate value and action. Once we make the judgment that our proposed course of action is the more valuable thing to do, the final step is deciding to do it. And all of this builds on the prior loop of operations where understanding and judgment are mobilized to investigate, understand, and verify the facts of the situation. Through it all, time and again through the process, the mind flips back and forth between the two loops, returning frequently to the data of experience for its resources. Authors who take this approach find the double loop model especially helpful for practitioners in fields like conflict and management.

Throughout the modules of this chapter, the puzzle exercises focus on the operations of the first loop, the operations of experiencing, understanding, and verifying matters of fact. The questions that dominate through the puzzle solving are the questions "What is it?" and "Is it so?" You are finished with the puzzle word when you gain the direct insight and then make the judgment that verifies that it is indeed a correct solution for this puzzle. The advantage of beginning with the threefold structure of the first loop is that scramble word puzzles provide a good laboratory for learning the skills for observing the operations of your mind. This path of skill development is carried forward in chapter 4, where modules 7–9 investigate the operations of the second loop, the operations involving feelings, values, and decisions. The point of entry into this second loop is the investigation of feelings. And the modules of chapter 4 explore how the two loops of operations work together in your problem-solving and your relationships.

MODULE 5: IDENTIFYING THE OPERATION OF DIRECT INSIGHT

To this point, in modules 3 and 4, you have practised skills for shifting your attention back and forth between your objects of consciousness and your mind's operations, as well as for differentiating groups of operations. You have done this by using a specific procedure for solving scramble words, the procedure of module 2.

In module 4, you practised focusing on how your mind groups diverse operations towards two specific goals: the goal of understanding that is achieved with direct insight, and the goal of verification that is achieved in judgment. Judgment involves a different kind of insight and is sometimes called reflective insight. Module 5 builds on these skills by focusing on the operation of direct insight.

MODULE 5: IDENTIFYING THE OPERATION OF DIRECT INSIGHT

Goals of This Module

- To begin developing skills for recognizing the operation of direct insight when it occurs in puzzle solving and in everyday life
- To begin developing your attention to and understanding of some of the distinctive features of direct insight

Instructions

For each day's activity, prepare your sheets of paper with scramble words as you have done for prior modules. Make sure you set all other concerns and interruptions aside and practise the activities alone, with no cell phones, tablets, or computers within attention range.

This week you will also need a second sheet of paper each day for recording your observations. Prepare your worksheet with the title "What My Mind Is Doing," as well as the module number and date at the top.

After you complete each scramble word, write down your observations on your worksheet. At the end of the week's sessions, read through your pages of observations and ask yourself what you have learned about your mind's operations from the scramble word sessions.

Your task this week is to work at solving the scramble words with a focus on what has just happened to you at the end of the second stage, in the moment before the third pause.

When you focus your observations on the operation of direct insight, make sure you locate your pause immediately after the insight and before engaging in the questioning for verification.

Suggestions and Questions

Here are some suggestions and questions for directing your observations:

1. You have likely noticed that the direct insight is a very difficult operation to observe. Pay attention to the way it comes as a surprise, catching you often unawares. Pay attention to this element of surprise and observe it recurring time and again in your puzzle solving. What can you observe about the difference between the operations you perform prior to the insight and the surprise occurrence of the insight itself?

2. You have likely noticed that the direct insight is a rapid-flash event that occurs very quickly, and it is easy to miss noticing its occurrence. Pay attention to each insight as it occurs and practise catching it, noticing it, and identifying the moment when it occurs. What can you say about the difficulty of catching this moment's occurrence? As you practise, can you observe yourself becoming more adept at noticing its occurrence?

3. You have likely observed that, because the insight event is such a rapid-flash operation (it seems to have little or no temporal magnitude), it seems rather difficult to describe its features. Consequently, in order to investigate this operation, think of it as a transformative operation that shifts your mind from a before-state to an after-state. Focus on this difference between your before-state and your after-state.

4. With respect to the scramble word, what can you observe about the difference between what is present to consciousness in the before-state and what is present to consciousness in the after-state? What has happened to you?

5. Throughout stage 2 of the puzzle solving, your mind has been directed or captured by the question, "What is it?"

What happens to this question once you shift from the before-state to the after-state? How would you describe the relationship between the question and the direct insight operation?
6   How would you describe the change in your state of feelings as you are transformed from the before-state to the after-state?
7   Insights occur frequently in life, and so it would be easy to think that we consider them familiar. But as you investigate insights, think about how strange they are. How do your observations challenge prior ways of thinking?
8   If someone who has never practised these exercises were to ask you to describe what happens to you as you practise this module, how would you answer them?

As in prior modules, you likely continue to observe positive or negative feelings related to performance anxiety, self-esteem, or competitive pressure arising, particularly when you encounter scramble words you have difficulty solving. Observe these feelings, but set them aside and focus on your mind's operations.

After the week's practice sessions, read over your observations and write a one-paragraph summary of what you have learned from your practice sessions. In your report, focus on your progress in achieving the goals of this week's activity rather than on the positive or negative feelings related to performance anxiety, self-esteem, or competitive pressure.

MODULE 6: IDENTIFYING THE OPERATION OF JUDGMENT

In module 4 you practised focusing on how your mind groups diverse operations. Module 5 built on these skills by focusing on direct insights. This module builds on these skills by focusing on the operation of judgment, also called the reflective insight. The aim is to observe some of the distinctive features of judgment and to better recognize this operation when it occurs in personal and professional life.

As with the direct insight, you are invited to pay attention to the distinctive pattern of questioning that sets you in motion towards the judgment, the strategies you use to gain the judgment, the emergence of the judgment itself, and the change in your state of consciousness that emerges when it occurs.

You will recall that verification involves a new type of questioning, a questioning that reflects on the insight and asks if it has the right features for you to judge it to be correct. In scramble words, you will notice that you count the letters and check to determine whether all the letters are accounted for. These are your questions for verification. When you can answer "yes" to all the questions, then your mind makes the judgment that your insight is correct.

This week's activity also involves writing down your daily observations and preparing a one-paragraph report.

MODULE 6: IDENTIFYING THE OPERATION OF JUDGMENT

Goals of This Module

- To begin developing skills for recognizing the operation of judgment when it occurs in puzzle solving and in everyday life
- To begin developing your attention to and understanding of some of the distinctive features of the operation of judgment

Instructions

For each day's activity, prepare your sheets of paper with scramble words as you have done in prior modules. Make sure you set all other concerns and interruptions aside and practise the activities alone, with no cell phones, tablets, or computers within attention range.

This week you will also need a second sheet of paper each day for recording your observations. Prepare your worksheet with the title "What My Mind Is Doing," the module number, and the date at the top.

The operation of judgment occurs at the end of the third stage, in the moment immediately prior to the fourth and final pause. After you complete each scramble word, write down your observations on your worksheet.

During stage 2, it is normal to gain a number of direct insights and then quickly examine and discard them. If you find this recurring, this is fine. If not, this is fine, too. If you do, after a few trials, you often settle into a longer period of wrestling with the puzzle word in search of a more novel candidate. When you make the breakthrough that discovers this more novel candidate, you often find that the verification process of stage 3 proves successful. For the purposes of this module, do not spend time trying to observe the many verification operations you perform quickly at the beginning of stage 2. Instead, focus on the operations your mind performs towards the end, after the longer period that leads to the more novel direct insight.

The judgment involves a different type of insight and is sometimes called the reflective insight. This is because it is an operation that reflects back on the direct insight. You have observed that once you gain the direct insight, your mind immediately engages in a new line of questioning about it. Focus on this group of operations that your mind rushes to perform after gaining the direct insight. Focus on what emerges in your consciousness that finally brings the process to completion.

Suggestions and Questions
Here are some questions and suggestions that can guide your observations:

1. After gaining the direct insight, notice the different type of questioning that your mind immediately launches. What are some differences between this questioning and the questioning that animates your mind during stage 2?
2. When your mind asks a particular question about the direct insight, what action does it invite you to perform in order to answer this question?
3. Pay careful attention to the final operation that your mind performs, the operation that brings this question-answer process to completion. What happens to your state of consciousness when your mind performs this final operation?
4. You have already observed some of the feelings that frequently accompany this final state. Observe these feelings. How are they similar to and different from the feelings that were present in you prior to the performance of the final operation?

As in prior modules, you likely continue to observe positive or negative feelings related to performance anxiety, self-esteem, or competitive pressure arising, particularly when you encounter scramble words you have difficulty solving. Observe these feelings, but set them aside and focus on your mind's operations.

After the week's practice sessions, read over your observations and write a one-paragraph summary of what you have learned from your practice sessions. In your report, focus on your progress in achieving the goals of this week's activity rather than on the positive or negative feelings related to performance anxiety, self-esteem, or competitive pressure.

APPLYING THE SKILLS

After completing module 6, your skill development process should be underway. At this point, you should be able to begin observing direct insights and judgments in everyday life. Notice, however, that the key word is "begin." Doing this is still difficult. Your mind continues to snap back quickly to its normal state. Your focus remains directed towards the objects of these operations, and it is difficult to pay attention to the operations themselves when they occur.

During the next few weeks, try focusing on direct insights. A good way to make progress in applying the skills is to choose activities where direct insights stand out. One of these is jokes. Pay attention to jokes and seek out people and places where jokes occur more frequently. Notice what happens to your mind when you "get" the joke. Notice the shift in the state of your mind from the "before" to the "after." Getting a joke involves the operation of direct insight. Pay attention and notice each insight as it occurs. Notice the various features of the direct insight that you recorded in your observations and report.

Another activity where you can notice direct insights is in some game shows.[5] Pay attention to the direct insights that occur in you as you work alongside the game show participants. Notice the "before-to-after" transformation that occurs in you with each direct insight. Notice how you feel when your mind performs this operation. You can also notice your insights in other puzzle types.

If you happen to be a person who likes fixing things, you can notice your direct insights by paying attention to what happens to you as you figure out what's wrong and how to fix it.[6] The expression "figure out" is another way of speaking about direct insights. You are confronted with a problem, you puzzle your way through, and at some point you hit on a possible solution. "Aha!" This is your direct insight. Pause after it occurs and notice it. To be sure, you need to verify your insight by performing the operation of judgment. Notice this too. Notice some of the features of the two operations that you have recorded in your notes and report.

If you followed the instructions at the end of chapter 2, you may have had some success in applying the skills in conversations. If so, you could build on this success by applying the skills from modules 4–6 in conversations. Try starting by focusing on the new insights you gain when you are deliberately curious about the meaning another person is expressing.

A normal way of engaging in conversations is to assume we already know what another person is saying. Often, while they are speaking, our minds shift away from them and focus on what we want to say next. Notice this attitude and deliberately replace it with a new attitude in which you turn your mind's focus back to the words they are saying. Remind yourself that you do not already understand the meaning they are trying to express. Likely there is some aspect you have missed. Mobilize the operation of questioning. Wonder about their meaning. Ask about it. Perhaps you could ask for clarification or an illustration. At some point, you will gain a direct insight. When this happens, pause and notice it. Notice what just happened to you. Notice the transition from the "before-to-after." To be sure, you will want to verify whether your insight is correct. When you do, notice how this changes the course of the conversation.

As your skills develop, so too will your expectations. Make sure you keep reminding yourself of your achievements. Keep the comparison with musical performance in mind. After six weeks of violin lessons, your performance abilities would likely be quite limited. Remind yourself that your impatience about future progress is a sign of past progress achieved.

CHAPTER FOUR

Feelings, Values, and Decisions: Practice Modules 7–9

In chapters 2 and 3, you focused on the basic skills for self-knowing and critical thinking, and you used these skills to identify some features of the operations of direct insight and judgment. Your goal was to develop skills for solving scramble word puzzles in a calm, measured way that allowed you to focus on the operations your mind performs in the solving process. Throughout the modules, you practised a special procedure for solving scramble word puzzles, a procedure that invited you to set aside your feelings of competitive pressure or performance anxiety. In these next modules, instead of setting aside these feelings, you are invited to focus on them. Your feelings play a role in your mind's operations, and in the modules of this chapter, you begin exploring this role.

The chapter begins with module 7, and here you begin working with more difficult puzzles in order to provide opportunities for feelings of competitive pressure or performance anxiety to arise. Module 7 is followed by a section titled "Excursus: Revisiting the Theory of Knowing." This section reconnects with the "Excursus" section of chapter 3 and offers an explanation that situates your feelings in relation to what some scholars call the "upper loop" of cognitional operations. This is the loop of operations in which your direct insights and judgments pursue values rather than facts. This is the loop of operations in which your decisions set you in motion to act on these values.

At first glance, it may seem that scramble word puzzles would not be helpful for exploring feelings, values, decisions, and actions. After all, puzzles like scramble words do not involve wrestling with important life decisions. On closer scrutiny, however, there are moments in everyone's puzzle solving when feelings arise and operations of decision come into play. Sometimes these moments can be dramatic. One notable example is the moment when you wrestle with feelings of competition or performance anxiety. You may not be thinking about this at the time, but these feelings are indeed occasions for life decisions. Your puzzle solving is part of a course of studies, and you may be paying for this course. You are taking this course to pursue a path of intellectual, professional, or personal development. Your decision to either quit or stay is indeed a life decision about the value of the course as part of this life development path. Your feelings function as links to this wider context. To launch this line of exploration, module 7 invites you to notice and explore these feelings and the values they evoke.

To be sure, this module marks a departure from the path you have been pursuing. So, at first, this module may seem odd. Your feelings of competitive pressure or performance anxiety are not tools your mind uses to solve scramble words. There is, however, a role your feelings do play. Your feelings require you to decide whether it is worthwhile to remain engaged with the puzzle and the self-knowing process. This brings a value judgment and a decision into play in the solving process. In addition, observing obvious feelings is a good way to begin investigating values and decisions, and this can help you observe value judgments and decisions that are not so obvious. Once you gain skills for observing decisions, you will notice that you do indeed make many small decisions throughout the puzzle solving process. And as you gain skills, you notice how feelings and values are indeed involved often in the process, notably when you feel good about success.

MODULE 7: IDENTIFYING FEELINGS AND VALUES

Previously, the instructions for the modules asked you to set aside your feelings of competition or performance anxiety. You have done this in order to focus on your operations of direct insight and judgment. Now you are invited to do something different. Instead of setting aside these feelings, you are invited to notice them, focus on them, and explore them in order to understand how they place you on a path towards value, decision, and action.

For this module, you will need to gather together two groups of puzzle words. For the first group, select puzzle words that are at the same level of difficulty as the ones you have been solving in previous modules. These should be puzzles that take more than fifteen seconds but less than three minutes to solve. For the second group, select puzzle words that are more difficult than the ones you have been solving. The puzzle words in this group should all take you more than three minutes to solve. It is possible that you will find puzzle words in this group that you cannot solve at all. If so, this is acceptable.

When practising this module, alternate back and forth between one puzzle word from the first group and one puzzle word from the second group. Begin by working with a puzzle word at your level. When you finish, select a more difficult puzzle word from the second group and work on it until your three minutes are up. Next, set this puzzle word aside and go back to working with an easier puzzle word from the first group. Then, select a brand new difficult puzzle word from the second group. Work with it for three minutes, then set it aside and go back to working with a new word from the easier group. Keep alternating back and forth for the rest of your practice sessions. Make sure that each time you work with a more difficult puzzle word it is a brand new word, not one of the words you have worked on previously. Keep alternating back and forth between easier and more difficult puzzle words for the rest of the week.

If you develop your skills so you can solve your more difficult puzzle words in less than three minutes, select new puzzle words that are more difficult. It is important that you continue alternating between puzzle words you can solve in your three-minute time period and puzzle words you cannot solve in your three-minute time period.

The instructions for this module invite you to pay attention to the feelings that arise when you are working with the difficult puzzle words from the second group.

MODULE 7: IDENTIFYING FEELINGS AND VALUES

Gather together two groups of puzzle words. For the first group, select puzzle words that are at the same level of difficulty as the ones you have been solving in previous modules. These should be scramble words that take more than fifteen seconds but less than three minutes to solve. For the second group, select scramble words that are more difficult than the ones you have been solving to date. The puzzle words in this group should take you more than three minutes to solve.

Goals of This Module

- To observe and examine the feelings of competitive pressure or performance anxiety that arise when you are unable to solve a puzzle word within the three-minute time period
- To begin observing how these feelings incline you towards action
- To begin exploring the values that are evoked in these feelings

Instructions

For each day's activity, prepare your materials as you have done in prior modules, and prepare your two groups of puzzle words. Make sure you set all other concerns and interruptions aside and practise the activities alone, with no cell phones, tablets, music, or computers within attention range.

This week you will also need a second sheet of paper each day for recording your observations. Prepare your worksheet with the title "What My Mind Is Doing," the module number, and the date at the top.

In solving your puzzle words, alternate back and forth between one easier puzzle word and one more difficult puzzle word. Focus your attention on the feelings that arise as you work with the more difficult puzzle word. When you shift back to the easier puzzle word, use the time to relax and shift out of the feelings evoked in working with the more difficult word.

When the feeling arises, pause the solving process and notice the feeling, observe it, ask what it is about, and ask how it orients or inclines you towards action. After you complete each scramble word, write down your observations on your worksheet.

Suggestions and Questions
Here are some questions and suggestions to guide you in observing and examining your feelings:

1 Notice whether the feeling is positive or negative. Try to describe the feeling in a few words.
2 Does the feeling incline or urge you towards some sort of action? If so, what sort of action?
3 If the feeling is positive, does it attract you towards something? If so, what?
4 If the feeling is negative, does it involve some sort of threat to something you care about? If so, what is the threat and what is the care that is threatened?

After the week's practice sessions, read over your observations and write a one-paragraph summary of what you have learned from your practice sessions. In your report, focus on your progress in achieving this week's goals.

EXCURSUS: REVISITING THE THEORY OF KNOWING

Before moving on to the next module, this section reconnects with the "Excursus" section of chapter 3 and offers some information that may help you understand the rationale behind the modules. If learners are eager to read more about Lonergan's philosophy, you are reminded that a good companion text would be Patrick Byrne's *The Ethics of Discernment*.

As noted in chapter 3, this approach to self-knowing provides a method for observing how your mind groups together various operations in order to achieve goals that build upon each other. Your sensory operations of seeing, hearing, tasting, smelling, and touching provide you with data that evoke questions for understanding. Your questioning, wondering, imaging, and trial-and-error puzzling head towards the goal of understanding that emerges in the operation of direct insight. The direct insight, however, is only a possible answer to your question. Consequently, once the direct insight emerges, your mind launches into the performance of questions and operations for verification. The goal of verification is achieved when your mind is satisfied that the relevant questions have been answered and you can pronounce a "yes" in the operation of judgment.

In simple puzzles, these three sets of operations bring closure to the process. In real life, however, your puzzles require that you act on your solutions. Also, your puzzle solving is part of a course of studies, and this course forms part of a path of intellectual, professional, or personal development you have decided to pursue. So, at every step along the way, you have been deciding whether or not to continue with this course as part of your development path. This means you have been deciding throughout the solving process.

When questions for decision and action arise, your mind moves into a second group of operations in which your questions for understanding and judgment are not "fact" questions; rather, they are "value" questions.[1] These value questions head you towards actions that are worthwhile, and they arise from and build on the answers to your fact questioning. For example, when you review your bank statement and verify that it has a mistaken charge on it, your mind shifts and begins asking, "What should I do?" Moreover, your mind is not satisfied with doing just anything. You need to know whether a proposed solution is truly valuable. Is it workable? Does it actually solve the problem? Is it fair or honest? Does the solution and its costs fit within a scale of values? Is your scale of values true or distorted? These are the operations of the upper loop, the operations that head towards judgments of value and decisions to act.

In all of this questioning, your feelings are evoked. Sometimes these feelings get in the way of clear thinking. But sometimes your feelings play a positive role in your clear thinking. This is because some types of feelings orient you to values and make these values present to your mind in ways that help you understand and assess them.[2] Often feelings orient you towards values that previously you had not known you held. Feelings can make these values present in ways that are quite new to you. Once present to your mind, you begin asking questions for understanding and value judgment in new ways.

In the scramble word modules, when your feelings of performance anxiety arise, they have the effect of inclining you towards value, decision, and action: perhaps to buckle down and try harder, perhaps to quit and walk away, perhaps to cheat, or perhaps to rail against the instructor. To be sure, you may decide not to follow up on one or another of these inclinations. But if so, notice that you have made a decision in light of a value or some candidate posing as a value. The goal of the module is to help you notice the way the feelings work in you to incline you towards value and decision. Once you notice this, you can reflect on the value and ask questions for understanding, judgment, and decision. What value is attracting me in the positive feeling? What value is being threatened in the negative feeling? Once you identify this value, you can assess it and ask about its suitability for decision and action. In this course, the problem you are solving is not simply the scramble word problem; rather, it is also the larger challenge of taking responsibility for the course as part of your intellectual, professional, or personal development path.

Throughout all the operations of your mind's two loops, the most noticeable mode of your mind's performance is questioning. Questioning moves your mind in pursuit of the object of each operation, and it moves you from one operation to another. In the modules of this chapter, you begin observing the different forms your questioning takes when it shifts from fact questions to value questions. You begin observing the distinctive form your questioning takes when you ask about your feelings. You begin observing the different form your questioning takes when it shifts into deliberation and decision. This means that questioning is your most reliable resource for helping you become more careful, more deliberate, and more responsible in life. Gaining familiarity with the different forms of questioning can help you along this path.

There is a great deal that can be said about the different forms that questioning takes when you move from one type of operation to another. For the present, I will offer a short summary and invite you to consult your companion text for further explanation. When you are working towards understanding facts, your questions ask, "What?" You want to know what something is, what happened, what makes something work. On the other hand, when you shift over to the operation of verification, your questioning focuses on the object of understanding and asks, "Is it so?" Here, your questioning is not answered by understanding something else. Rather, it is answered by a "yes" or a "no." Often, your best answer is "I don't know." But this only invites you to dig deeper into the actions required for reaching a "yes" or "no" judgment.

When you move into what we've called the upper loop of operations, your mind shifts again, this time to questions that ask, "What to do?" Notice, however, that the "what" in this case is not simply about whether an action is possible. Your questioning also contains questions about what is worthwhile, what is worth doing, and what is the best thing to do. Here is where your feelings come in. Once you arrive at answers to these questions, your mind shifts again to ask whether you've got it right. Again, your question for judgment asks, "Is it so?" This time, the questioning asks whether the action is truly valuable, whether it is actually or only apparently the best option, and whether you are being responsible or short-sighted in your thinking and planning. Finally, your mind shifts to the question for action. This is the question about putting your judgment into action. This is the question that is answered by acting.

In this Insight studies course, modules 7 and 8 offer a very limited introduction to the upper loop of operations involving feelings, values, and decisions. There is a great deal more to be learned. These two modules provide a small sample of resources that are developed further by authors such as Patrick Byrne in *The Ethics of Discernment*. What you can do, however, is practise the skills you have learned in everyday life contexts. The final section of this chapter, "Applying the Skills," offers suggestions for doing this.

MODULE 8: FEELINGS, VALUES, AND DECISIONS

The goal of this module is to help you observe and examine the links between your feelings, values, and decisions. In the prior module, you paused in the solving process and noticed your feelings of competition or performance anxiety, and you began exploring the values that are evoked in your feelings. In this module, you build on this skill and explore: (a) how your feelings incline you in the direction towards values, (b) how your value judgments either affirm or reject this direction, and (c) how your value judgments incline you towards decisions to act on your judgments.

In the prior module, you paused and observed your mind asking questions to understand the value evoked in your feelings. In this module, understanding the value is not your main concern. Often your mind makes judgments about values evoked in feelings before understanding them. To be sure, using your mind responsibly requires pausing to understand your values. The goal of this module, however, is to take the next step and observe the links between your feelings, value judgments, and decisions.

In this module, you will find the word "incline" in the instructions. You will be invited to observe how your mind's operations incline you in certain directions: towards the goal of the operation, towards the performance of other operations, or towards a broader goal that you seek to achieve in your decisions and actions. One of the goals of the module is to become familiar with this experience of being "inclined." You will observe the way your feelings incline you in certain directions. But you will also observe the way your mind's operations incline you in certain directions, and you will observe how the completion of one operation inclines you towards the next operation. You will observe the way success in completing one scramble word often inclines you towards starting another puzzle.

In this module, you will continue using two sets of scramble words as you did in the previous module. Throughout the week's practice sessions, continue alternating back and forth between one easier scramble word and one more difficult puzzle word. Observe any competitive or performance anxiety feelings arising in either the easier or more difficult scramble words.

MODULE 8: FEELINGS, VALUES, AND DECISIONS
Gather together two groups of puzzle words. For the first group, select puzzle words that are at the same level of difficulty as the ones you have been solving in previous

modules. These should be scramble words that take more than fifteen seconds but less than three minutes to solve. For the second group, select scramble words that are more difficult than the ones you have been solving to date. The puzzle words in this group should take you more than three minutes to solve.

Focus on any competitive or performance anxiety feelings arising in either the easier or more difficult scramble words.

Goals of This Module

- To observe and explore how your feelings of competitive pressure or performance anxiety incline you in the direction towards values
- To observe and explore how these feelings incline you towards value judgments
- To observe and explore how your value judgments either affirm or reject the direction evoked in your feelings
- To observe and explore how your value judgments incline you towards decisions to act on your judgments

Instructions

For each day's activity, prepare your materials as you have done in prior modules, and prepare your two groups of puzzle words. Make sure you set all other concerns and interruptions aside and practise the activities alone, with no cell phones, tablets, music, or computers within attention range.

This week you will also need the second sheet of paper each day for recording your observations. Prepare your worksheet with the title "What My Mind Is Doing," the module number, and the date at the top.

In solving your puzzle words, alternate back and forth between one easier puzzle word and one more difficult puzzle word. Focus your attention on any feelings of competitive pressure or performance anxiety arising as you work with puzzle words in either group.

When the feeling of competitive pressure or performance anxiety arises, pause the solving process and notice the feeling. Observe how it inclines you in a direction towards some sort of operation or action.

Suggestions and Questions
Here are some questions and suggestions to guide you in observing and examining your feelings:

1 When the feeling is positive, observe how it inclines you or attracts you towards something.
2 When the feeling is negative, observe how it inclines you away from something, often to preserve or protect something else.
3 Notice that the feeling inclines you towards making a judgment about the direction evoked in the feeling.
4 Notice that your mind raises and answers questions in order to make this value judgment.
5 Notice that the value judgment inclines you towards decision and action.
6 Notice that sometimes you decide to act against your better judgment. Notice how you feel when you do this.

After the week's practice sessions, read over your observations and write a one-paragraph summary of what you have learned from your practice sessions. In your report, focus on your progress in achieving this week's goals.

MODULE 9: OBSERVING AN INNER NORMATIVITY

This is the last module of the course, and in a certain way, it is an invitation for you to reflect back on the observations you have made in all eight prior modules. This reflection, however, is also an invitation into a new line of questioning that builds on your observations from module 8. You are invited to observe the way that each and every one of your mind's operations inclines you in two ways: (a) towards its own goals, and (b) towards the next operation in the sequence. To be sure, this sequence is not necessarily a time sequence. Your mind often jumps around among operations. But as it does, it also assembles its achievements in a pattern that could be called cumulative or developing. In this case, the sequence is more of a building sequence than a temporal sequence. For example, in order to build towards a good value judgment, your mind needs to understand and verify the facts of the situation.

This pattern of inclinations is what can be called your mind's "inner normativity." Lonergan scholars use the term "self-transcending" to speak of this inner normativity.[3] To transcend is to go beyond, and going beyond implies some sort of development that builds on a past achievement and enables a new achievement. The term "normative" implies a direction for action that you should be following, a direction like a compass point. In this case, the compass pointing is this developmental pattern that is built into the very structure of your mind. Your mind follows this direction in self-assembling the operations, but it does its work best when you understand and value its pointing and make decisions to follow its pointing.

This is not a normativity you simply learn from others. Rather it arises from within the very structure of your mind. It can be reinforced by others, but it is not put there by others. In fact, it is the very basis of your learning from others. If you learn something from others, it is only by using this inner normativity of your mind. The structure and direction of this inner normativity is one of building and correcting. At each step in the process, you go beyond the prior step by building and correcting, and it is this notion of "going beyond" and developing that is captured by the term "normative." The goal of this final module is to observe this inner normativity at work in the various stages of the solving process.

MODULE 9: OBSERVING AN INNER NORMATIVITY

In this module, continue working with your two groups of scramble words. Gather together two groups of puzzle words. For the first group, select puzzle words that are at the same level of difficulty as the ones you have been solving in previous modules. These should be scramble words that take more than fifteen seconds but less than three minutes to solve. For the second group, select scramble words that are more difficult than the ones you have been solving to date. The puzzle words in this group should take you more than three minutes to solve.

Goals of This Module

- To observe how each of your mind's operations inclines you towards its own goal
- To observe how each of your mind's operations also inclines you towards the next operation in the building sequence when it achieves its own goal
- To observe how each operation goes beyond or transcends the achievements of the prior operations and carries you along this path of step-by-step self-transcending
- To observe how these inclinations self-assemble into an overall pattern that can be described as an "inner normativity"

Instructions

For each day's activity, prepare your materials as you have done in prior modules, and prepare your two groups of puzzle words. Make sure you set all other concerns and interruptions aside and practise the activities alone, with no cell phones, tablets, music, or computers within attention range.

This week you will also need the second sheet of paper each day for recording your observations. Prepare your worksheet with the title "What My Mind Is Doing," the module number, and the date at the top.

In solving your puzzle words, alternate back and forth between one easier puzzle word and one more difficult puzzle word.

As you work through the easier scramble words, observe what your mind is inclining you to do in each of the four pauses.

When working with puzzle words from the second, more difficult group, pause when feelings of competition or performance anxiety arise. Observe what your mind is inclining you to do.

When working with puzzle words from the first, easier group, give special attention to the fourth pause. Observe what your mind inclines you to do after successfully completing the scramble word.

Suggestions and Questions

Here are some questions and suggestions to guide you in your observations:

1 During the first pause, observe how "seeing" immediately inclines your mind towards the questions for understanding. Observe how difficult it is to resist this inclining.

2 During the second pause, observe how your mind inclines you back into the solving process. Notice how difficult it is to resist this inclining.

3 During the second pause, notice how your mind tries out various solving strategies. Notice that each time you try out a strategy, you are making a decision. Notice how strongly your mind inclines you towards making these strategy decisions.

4 When working with scramble words from the second, difficult group, observe the feelings of competition and performance anxiety that arise. Notice how they incline

you towards a decision, either to quit or to stay. When you feel like quitting, notice the pull or inclination of the feeling even when you decide not to quit. Notice how your mind also inclines you in another direction, towards the broader value that you affirm in the judgment when you decide not to quit.
5 When working with scramble words from the first, easier group, during the third pause, observe the way your direct insight, once achieved, immediately inclines you towards the operation of verification.
6 When working with scramble words from the first group, during the fourth pause, observe the feeling of satisfaction that arises with your mind's successful performance of the final operation of verification. Notice how this final operation, and the feelings it evokes, often inclines you towards starting a new puzzle.
7 Notice how you are getting better at performing the skills of self-observation. Notice how this "getting better" is a step-by-step process of self-transcending.
8 Notice how you are using the inner normativity of your mind's operations to observe, understand, verify, and appropriate the inner normativity of your mind's operations.

After the week's practice sessions, read over your observations and write a one-paragraph summary of what you have learned from your practice sessions. In your report, focus on your progress in achieving this week's goals.

APPLYING THE SKILLS

Completing module 9 brings you to the end of the practice modules of this introductory course in Insight studies. At this point, you should be developing your self-knowing abilities, your ability to observe your mind performing various operations from time to time in everyday life. To be sure, the course is introductory and your skills remain limited. Your mind continues to snap back to its normal focus on the objects of your operations. It is still difficult for you to notice and remain focused on the operations themselves. Yet, in working through the nine modules of the course, you have made progress. If you continue practising the skills, this path of progress can continue long after the course ends.

A good way to apply the skills you have learned is to ask, "Have I skipped a step?"[4] This is one of the most common ways we fall down in our efforts to be responsible friends, colleagues, and citizens. We gain an insight, but we skip over verifying it. We verify a fact, but then we rush directly to a decision without examining or assessing our values. We take responsibility for implementing a course of action, but we fail to ask whether we have understood the situation properly. We find ourselves in situations that evoke strong value feelings, but we fail to assess whether the values evoked are appropriate.

During the next few weeks, try focusing on situations where you need to diagnose a problem and implement a solution.[5] It could be an auto repair problem, a home repair problem, or a health care problem. It could be a relationship problem, or it could be a childcare logistics problem. It could be a problem at home, or it could be a problem in the workplace. Ideally, choose a time when the problem is not so urgent that you must act immediately. To practise your skills, you need to be able to take the time to shift your focus of attention back and forth between your problem-solving and your self-knowing.

Start by noticing the operations you perform in diagnosing the problem. These are the operations of direct insight and judgment that you identified in modules 5 and 6. These are the operations involved in observing, understanding, and verifying the facts of the problem. Notice that when you seek to understand the problem, you also seek to understand something about why or how it happened. As you probe the problem, notice your mind raising and answering the questions for understanding and verification. Notice how your mind constantly returns to consult the data in order to make the judgments that verify your insights. Notice how your mind does not accept your insights as reliable knowledge until you have asked and answered the questions for verification. Keep asking the question: "Have I skipped a step?"

Once you gain some understanding of the problem, notice your mind asking the next set of questions: "What should I do?" At this point, you shift into the operations of understanding and verifying the values that move you towards decision and action. Notice the feelings that arise in you and ask what your feelings are about. What values are they evoking in you? Are the values relevant to the situation? Are they reliable? Do they solve the problem? Do they do so fairly? Do the costs fit within your scale of values? Is your scale of values reliable, or have you noticed troubling distortions? Keep asking the question: "Have I skipped a step?"

Notice that sometimes, as you gather data for your value judgments, you discover that your understanding of the problem is inadequate or incomplete. Notice that, at these moments, your mind takes you back to the first loop of operations, your questions for understanding and judgments about the facts of the situation. Notice that when your mind is working properly, you shift back and forth between the two loops of operations. Notice how the process comes to completion when you make the decision to implement the solution. Notice how you often implement the solution with an eye towards further verification. Notice that when you discover you've missed something, you restart the process and work to implement corrections, perhaps in a future situation.

If you followed the instructions at the end of chapters 2 and 3, you have done some important work applying the skills in conversations. You can build on this work by applying this same set of problem-solving questions to your conversations. Keep asking yourself: "Have I skipped a step?" After module 6, you began asking this question when you paused to consider whether you had understood the other person correctly. Now you can apply what you have learned about feelings and values to investigate the role your own feelings sometimes play in blocking or skewing your understanding of their intended meaning.

Sometimes in conversations, your mind gets blocked or biased in understanding others when their words or gestures evoke feelings of threat. These feelings are often difficult to notice, and they are even more difficult to explain. But their effect can be dramatic.[6] When you feel that something valuable is threatened, your mind constricts to focus resolutely on defending against an expected attack. When this happens, the first thing that gets truncated is your questioning.

Your mind immediately stops mobilizing the questioning required for understanding and verifying their intended meaning. In place of this, your feelings fill your mind with images of them as some sort of foe. You become certain you will be harmed. The questioning you pursue is towards mobilizing a defence.

In such cases, once you notice this happening, your Insight skills can help you pause and ask, "Have I skipped a step?" Of course, the answer is "yes." You have skipped the operation of verification, the judgment of fact. You have failed to ask whether your understanding of their intended meaning is correct. In place of the questioning that would help you gain a better understanding of them and the situation, your feeling of threat has moved you directly into decision and action to defend against threat.[7] Your goal, then, is to deliberately decide to go back to the operation you skipped. This is not easy to do. But it is possible with practice. And your Insight skills can help you value the practice of remaining attentive to "skipping steps."

To be sure, threats are often real. Yet real threats, like all other problems, require the correct understanding of others and situations if they are to be faced responsibly. They also require the correct understanding of ourselves and our feelings. All this requires performing all the operations of both loops. And it requires mobilizing the operations that investigate and assess the values evoked in feelings. This means practice in remaining attentive to "skipping steps."

The next chapter, "Applications," offers six short summaries of authors' works that provide further insights into directions for applying the skills. The disciplines chosen for these applications are ethics, conflict studies, sociology, psychology, philosophy, and politics. In each case, the authors have learned and practised the skills you have begun developing in this course. They show how the skills can make a difference in pursuing the questions of their discipline. I would like to conclude by suggesting that your own path of skill development places you in a privileged position for understanding and appreciating their contributions. At every step along the way, they are speaking about operations of the mind that you have experienced, understood, and verified. You are in a good position to know what they are talking about. And you are in a good position to share their interest in the contributions Insight studies can make to their discipline.

CHAPTER FIVE

Applications

The six authors surveyed in this chapter have been chosen because they not only draw on the work of Lonergan; they also apply the methods and skills of self-knowing to diverse disciplines. Lonergan wrote most of his works as contributions to theology. But their relevance has been found to reach far beyond theology. Scholars working in such fields as economics, business, physics and evolutionary science, environmental studies, urban studies, nursing, and education have drawn on Lonergan to enhance their work.[1] And the authors surveyed here offer their works as contributions to ethics, conflict studies, sociology, psychology, philosophy, and politics.

My focus in these surveys is on the relevance of the self-knowing and critical thinking skills you have learned in the practice-based approach of Insight studies. In each case, the author presents and develops novel insights that arise from *doing* self-knowing. Most students who study Lonergan read his works. Yet Lonergan himself tells his readers they cannot understand his works by simply reading his works. They must be *doing* something as they read. This something is implementing the skills. To do this, they must learn how to do this. In this Insight studies course, you have taken the first and most important step along this learning path. You have begun learning how to do what you must do if you want to understand this body of work. This means you are now in a privileged position to begin understanding the novel contributions offered by the authors surveyed here.

There is another reason why these authors have been chosen. Their works focus on life skills. They may emerge from particular disciplines, but they are relevant beyond the limits of these disciplines. They are relevant to your day-to-day living. They deal with ethical issues you face as a person and citizen. They deal with conflicts you face in all areas of life. They deal with arguments that can harm your relationships. They deal with the problems you must solve at home and in the workplace. They deal with the big philosophical issues that can bring you to the edge of despair. They deal with the troubling questions that arise at the intersection of politics and religion.

What the authors bring to their disciplines arises from the learning path you have pursued in this course, the path of self-knowing and critical thinking. This means that each author also presents you with a possible direction for applying and developing your skills. I offer this survey in the hope that one or more of them might capture your interest and offer a compelling path forward.

ETHICS AND DISCERNMENT

As a retired university professor in the field of ethics, I am pleased to report that, in my thirty-five years of teaching, I have observed no shortage of women and men passionately dedicated to pursuing the good and righting the wrongs of the world. My concern, however, is with the resources my discipline has offered in service of these goals. If the daily news is a reliable indicator, ethics is in disarray. To be sure, public attention to ethical issues is high. The problem, however, is that there is little agreement within the discipline on how to approach the issues.

The main difficulty is not that people disagree on big ethical issues. It is that debates over issues give rise to debates over theories, methods, and approaches, and the discipline offers little guidance on how to navigate this field of challenges. Eventually, the very meanings of the words "ethical," "moral," "right," and "wrong" are called into question. Our inability to agree on the basics begins eroding our confidence in any effort to offer ethical judgments that could mobilize collective action on serious issues. This is troubling.

My first author in this survey offers a promising avenue for addressing these questions, an avenue that highlights the centrality of the skills you have begun learning. Patrick Byrne's book *The Ethics of Discernment* applies the skills of self-knowing to fundamental questions in ethics.[2] He offers readers a method for making ethical judgments that is both sensitive to context, culture, and diversity and solid in affirming an ethical objectivity needed for collective action. He can do this because objectivity, properly understood, can apply to diverse contexts and cultures when it is rooted in the mind's inner normativity.

His work follows the approach of Lonergan, and he uses the word "discernment" to speak about the method of self-knowing.[3] As you have learned in this course, what distinguishes the method is the focus, not on the prescriptions, rules, or formulations, but on a structure of operations at work in your mind as you experience, understand, evaluate, and act on ethical knowledge. The invitation is to embark on the fascinating journey of self-discovery, what Byrne calls the journey of discernment. We all live our daily lives engaged in acts of ethical experience, understanding, judgment, and decision. These acts have characteristics we can observe in ourselves. They have an inner normativity we can all come to know by attending to our minds' operations.

Byrne's book is structured as an effort to answer some difficult questions about ethics left unanswered in the writings of Lonergan. As the chapters unfold, however, readers find striking analyses that address major challenges arising in ethics today: tradition and diversity, subjectivity and objectivity, reason and religion, rationality and affectivity. These are challenges at the root of disagreements we encounter in public life. The fourth of these, rationality and affectivity, is a central concern of the book, and it takes up five of sixteen chapters.[4]

Lonergan never worked out a complete treatment of ethics, so Byrne takes the initial materials on ethics from *Insight* and develops them into a fully rounded analysis of ethical foundations by examining earlier and later primary and secondary texts and adding his own original contributions. He organizes the chapters by adapting for ethics a threefold line of questioning Lonergan uses for his own study of human understanding in *Insight*: What are we doing when we are being ethical? Why is doing that being ethical? And what is brought about by doing that? To introduce discernment, Byrne situates Lonergan in relation to three historical figures notable for their contributions to the topic: Aristotle, Paul of Tarsus, and Ignatius of Loyola.[5] To help readers engage in their own work of discernment, Byrne offers analyses of examples from literature, art, sports, philosophy, and everyday experience.

Unlike other authors who focus on ethical theories, arguments, or principles, Byrne draws on the method of self-appropriation to focus on the foundational role played by ethical questions. These questions arise spontaneously in our lives when we puzzle over what to do and whether an action is truly good. But cultivating a disciplined and methodical practice of ethical engagement requires attending carefully to the full range of questions that arise. Making responsible value judgments requires that we answer all the relevant questions. This means paying careful attention to these questions – all of them – even when we would normally brush some of them aside. There is a self-correcting process to this method, and it forces us eventually to push beyond the limitations of inadequate horizons, even when these horizons have become the culturally accepted norm. What Byrne helps us understand is that the driver of this self-correcting process arises in our questioning.[6]

In chapters 5–9, Byrne explores the role of feelings in ethics. Instead of thinking of ourselves as having separate faculties of reason and emotion, operating in different zones and yielding products that are so different they cannot be reconciled, he invites readers to discern specific types of feelings that introduce value-affects into the horizon of reason and reflection. Once present in consciousness, these value-affects shape the direction of our understanding and are taken up by operations of reflection and judgment that subject them to scrutiny in appeals to evidence.

It remains true there are diverse types of feelings, and some present obstacles to rational reflection. But other types of feelings, far from blocking or bypassing reasonable investigation and judgment, yield the distinctive value intentionality that is operative in ethical reflection; thus, the need for discernment to sort out types of feelings. This analysis champions the role of feelings in ethics but does not collapse into an emotivism that rejects rational foundations for ethics. Rather, Byrne finds the value-affects emerging with these types of feelings to be amenable to objective scrutiny.[7]

The theme of discernment is central because it pertains to both the pursuit of responsibility in ethical living and the scholarly study of ethics. As relevant to ethical living, discernment is cultivated as we develop and implement skills for attending to feelings and for evaluating their reliability in a responsible life. This is something we do already, but ethical maturity requires dedication to development. Byrne shows how it takes practice and is cultivated slowly and only partially through adult life. Discernment is also relevant to the scholarly study of ethics, where it becomes the method of self-appropriation that yields verified explanations of the operations of ethical living.

Chapters 11–14 link human subjectivity to an ethical world and a scale of values that can be affirmed as objective and open to transcendent love. The basis for objectivity, however, is not logic, propositions, frameworks, or traditions. Rather, it is a state of authenticity of human persons. Once again, the significance of discernment looms large. Byrne's original contribution here is his analysis of the scale of values in relation to Lonergan's emergent probability understanding of world process.[8] What unfolds is an objectivist ethics that remains modest in its claims about what questions have been settled objectively.

In my judgment, the book's most important contribution lies in chapters 15 and 16. Here he offers a method for examining and making judgments on ethical issues, a method based in what Lonergan calls the Functional Specialties. Ethics is not simply a matter of me reasoning alone in a vacuum. Rather, as in all areas of life, when something is important, I seek advice from people with expertise. In ethics, the women and men who can offer this advice are those who work together to develop historical studies of diverse ethical analyses on the issue. Their task is not simply to describe this history but to arrive at some measure of agreement on a dialectical analysis that traces a normative path forward. The historical-dialectical study examines both concrete judgments and the ethical theories and methods behind the judgments. The method traces a historical trajectory in which some questions have been resolved, some left open, some answers affirmed, some overturned and corrected, and some trajectories have emerged as most promising.[9]

The relevance of self-appropriation in this historical-dialectical method is best observed in the most important task arising in ethics, the dialectical task of sorting out conflicts rooted in the opposition between "positions" and "counter-positions." Here it is worth quoting Byrne:

> By "positions," Lonergan means statements that are not merely logically consistent with other statements, but are

also consistent with the actual performance of the structured activities of cognitional structure. By extension, we may speak of positions as statements that are consistent with the more encompassing structure of ethical intentionality. A statement such as "Objectivity in matters of fact and value is possible" would be an example of a position. Counter-positions are statements that are inconsistent with the exercise of ethical intentionality. For example, the assertion "It is always bad to make value judgments" would be of a counter-position, since the person making the statement is exercising the very activity she or he condemns.[10]

Byrne offers a way of doing ethics that identifies a basis for working through the conflicts arising in the diverse theories, methods, and traditions behind the issues. This basis is the inner normativity that is operative in the mind's own structure. Understanding and taking ownership of this inner normativity provides grounds for catching ourselves in making statements that bring us into conflict with our own inner normativity. This means that scholars and practitioners in ethics have an advantage when they have well-developed discernment skills.

What is interesting is the universality of Byrne's approach. The method of discernment can be implemented by anyone who has developed the abilities. This is important when conversations in democratic societies engage citizens from diverse and conflicting traditions. When ethical conflicts arise, participants cannot appeal to shared traditions or frameworks as a basis for decisions that impact us all. This is important when individual traditions encounter novel challenges that stretch the resources offered by past authorities. And it is important when traditions face the need to correct oversights and biases that have affected them. In all cases, participants in ethical conversations, when they have developed the relevant skills, can appeal to the basic normative framework offered by the structure of their own ethical intentionality. Their skills can help in discerning traces of the movement towards ethical authenticity in past histories of traditions – their own as well as others'. And the method proves reliable because, when practised authentically, it is both critical and self-critical. What Byrne offers is a method that goes to the heart of the matter. In so doing, he allows readers to catch a glimpse of a promising path forward. I would say this is no small achievement.

CONFLICT AND INSIGHT

The next author in this survey, Cheryl Picard, has been practising conflict mediation and training mediators since the early years when the discipline was getting established. Like many of her colleagues, she developed a successful practice before adopting a theory. When called on to explain her work, she and I co-directed a research team that worked out a theory of conflict and mediation rooted in Lonergan's self-appropriation. The result was Insight Mediation and the book, *Transforming Conflict through Insight.*[11]

Theorists and practitioners in the field of conflict are dedicated to understanding, practising, and teaching skills to help parties deal constructively with conflicts in diverse areas of life and work. One line of theory and practice in the field is mediation, a process designed to help parties work through conflicts. Mediators do not resolve conflicts. Rather, they facilitate conversations between conflicting parties with a view towards helping them work out their own solutions. Picard's work focuses on interpersonal and small group conflicts. Practising mediators are familiar with a moment in the mediation when parties shift out of an attitude of closure to one of openness to opportunities for resolution. She wanted to understand what was going on in these moments.

At the time, the various ways of explaining conflict and mediation tended to gather, roughly, into two groups: those that focused on problem-solving (interest theories) and those that focused on relationship-building (Transformative Mediation).[12] Of course, this is a simplification. But it does highlight a difference that is still recognized as important in the field. Interest theories tend to focus on problem-solving. For example, Roger Fisher argues that mediation is about solving problems and gaining agreements so that parties can get on with their lives.[13] His contribution has been to point out that conflicts are seldom about what parties argue about. Rather, behind the issues lie deeper interests that often have not been identified by the parties.

According to Fisher, parties in conflict focus resolutely on issues. These are things like contested amounts of money, child custody arrangements, disputed property, or conditions of employment. But often they focus on these issues without considering why, that is to say, the deeper reasons for holding onto positions in the dispute. Identifying these deeper reasons means probing for interests. Once interests are identified and articulated, parties are able to stand back and reflect more broadly on the issues. With the help of mediators, parties can recognize common interests, and this paves the way for negotiating ways of meeting the interests of all.

Interest theories have had an enormous influence, but they have also attracted considerable criticism. Critics argue they assume an overly narrow, individualistic understanding of the human person and an overly pragmatic theory of conflict. Conflicts are about more than problem-solving: they are about relationships, and dealing with relationships calls for a wider and deeper model of mediation.

One of the alternatives is the Transformative Mediation model of Robert Baruch Bush and Joseph Folger.[14] Transformative Mediation focuses on the relationships that arise from the communal character of human life. Mediators aim at nurturing or restoring relationships, and often this means cultivating occasions for moral growth and personal transformation. Like interest-based mediators, they believe mediation involves probing the dispute for underlying factors. But unlike interest-based mediators, they focus on "empowerment" and "recognition," key factors they believe will open doors to nurturing or restoring relationships. Transformative Mediation strategies are much less pragmatic and directive; they are more open and flexible. Mediators allow parties to explore diverse ranges of issues they believe may be relevant to the relationship.

To be sure, Transformative Mediation attracted its own critics. And in the years following, the development of more and more diverse mediation models and theories provided the occasion for considerable reflection on theories of conflict. In order to advance the training of mediators, practitioners needed to gain a clearer understanding of what they were doing and how it affected the conflict. This required theorists who could explain conflict and how it gets resolved. Some in the field, including Picard, remained dissatisfied with the dominant theories and looked elsewhere for resources. The result was a partnership between scholars and practitioners in conflict and Lonergan scholars interested in helping them with their work.[15]

Lonergan's work provided the research team with a novel way of investigating and explaining what happens in the minds of parties in conflict. The central element was provided by the method of self-knowing. Researchers placed themselves in conflict situations and examined their own minds' operations. Their discovery was that, contrary to popular thinking, conflict and conflict resolution need to be understood as learning.[16] Conflict involves blockages to the normal dynamism of questioning and curiosity that is central to navigating day-to-day relationships. This questioning is the basis for learning about others, and conflict blocks this process of learning. They discovered that the key to this blockage is the experience of feelings of threat.[17] When threatened, our minds become radically constricted. We become blocked in our ability to perform the operations involved in learning properly about the other person.

The focus of Insight Mediation is on the work the mediator does to facilitate parties' own learning. She helps them gain direct and reflective insights that open avenues for resolving problems and rebuilding relationships. This pursuit of insight is a learning process that goes on within conflicts, and understanding insight has proven helpful in explaining and advancing the learning that occurs when conflicts are resolved well. At the centre is Lonergan's analysis of the curious and transformative structure of insight itself. Insights must be pursued actively, but they must be received passively. Their occurrence can be made more probable, but it cannot be controlled. They are a transformative emergence that shifts the subject's entire world of understanding, feeling, valuing, and relating to others. Prior to insights, we cannot imagine them. After, we cannot recall our prior state of confusion. The formative insights in conflict are those that go to the heart of the threat feelings that block our learning about others.

Picard found that the method and framework of Insight not only explained her practice but also helped her develop it in novel directions. Her second book, *Practising Insight Mediation*, offers an expanded account of the elements and strategies involved in Insight Mediation. Learning about insight, mediators learn how better to "deepen the learning conversation" among the parties in the conflict.[18] They learn how to help parties move out of blockages created by threats and into a deeper understanding of the cares at the root of relationships. Mediators learn how to establish patterns of questioning that permit parties to listen and understand each other in new ways. They learn to avoid disrupting parties' learning by announcing diagnoses or solutions. They learn to become attuned to parties' body language as indicators of openness. They learn the difference between direct insights and the reflective insights or judgments that subject them to verification. They learn to remain forever open to parties' own learning paths.

Central to Insight Mediation is Lonergan's understanding of feelings and values.[19] Mediators probe feelings in order to help parties understand and articulate values underlying their words and actions. Values are not simply personal interests or possessions. They are patterns of social relations that link the past and present with futures and evoke expectations of progress or decline. Probing threat feelings to discover values, mediators help parties understand how their future expectations shape their ability to understand each other.

The turning point in Insight Mediation is the transformation in the conflict that arises when mediators help parties de-link from expectations of threat. Central to conflict is a conviction of necessity linking the other party's actions to my own feelings of threat. In relationships, this takes diverse forms. Your intelligence necessarily implies my stupidity. Your courage necessarily threatens my self-esteem. Ultimately, when conflicts become violent, your very existence threatens my family and my community. The conflict is driven not simply by the opposition of values, but by a conviction that your values necessarily threaten my own. As long as this expectation remains, I am compelled to reject the other's value to preserve my own.

What is most interesting about this situation is that as long as this expected intelligibility governs my participation in the conflict, I cannot be curious about the other's value. This means I will not understand it. To be sure, I can and often do become curious about strategies for attack or defence. But as long as I feel threatened, it is extremely difficult to give myself over to the genuine questioning that is the beginning of real learning. This means that conflicts lock parties in a state of darkness and ignorance about what really matters to everyone.

Mediators help parties break out of this state when they facilitate the direct and reflective insights that de-link the threat. When I verify that I have misunderstood something important, I discover that this expected link or intelligibility is not a necessity. It may have shaped the past, but the past need not determine the present or the future. Your intelligence need not imply my stupidity. Your courage need not have anything to say about my own self-worth. And a history of violence that has marked the interaction between persons or communities need not pronounce the last word on present or future possibilities. The present and future are liberated from bondage to the past. Moreover, using our minds responsibly liberates parties' curiosity about the values at the heart of the other's position. Relieved from the burden of protecting against threat, parties can, according to Picard, become curious about others and what matters to them.

SOCIOLOGY AND EVERYDAY ARGUMENTS

Marnie Jull trained as an Insight mediator in Cheryl Picard's program at Carleton University, and she went on to study interpersonal conflict using an innovative adaptation of the sociological method called autoethnography. Her book, *An Anatomy of Everyday Arguments*, offers readers an engaging analysis of four case studies and provides a fascinating example of how researchers can investigate their own minds' operations within the discipline of sociology.[20]

> Through my four cases, I experiment with and progressively develop a flexible, critical autoethnography. The cases are presented as vignettes through which I reflect on and systematically investigate my own subjectivity in relation to that of others. I explore the microprocesses of knowing and deciding that activate my actions in my roles as a partner, mother, friend, colleague, and so on.[21]

The book is structured in three parts. The first three chapters discuss various aspects of methodology. The next four chapters present and analyze the four case studies. And chapters 8 and 9 discuss the results and their implications for enquiry in sociology and conflict analysis. While the book may seem like a rather dry sociological study, readers find the writing, especially in the middle four chapters, to be lively, personal, and compelling. Most interesting for Insight studies is the direction Jull offers for pursuing self-knowledge within sociology.

Autoethnography is a sociological method in which researchers are involved as actors in the cases examined in the research. In Jull's adaptation, the sociological study of the cases calls for a reflexive self-examination on the part of the researcher as the case is studied. But it also incorporates the reflections of others involved in the case through "debriefing enquiries." As the research unfolds, researchers learn from both their own self-reflection and from their discussions with others, and the result is a "layered account" in which the steps in the learning are captured in the written account.[22]

Jull's focus in studying everyday arguments is on the change process in conflicts. Like Picard, she explores what is going on when conflict behaviour changes or shifts so that conflict dissipates, making room for new possibilities to emerge. Her framework for investigating conflict is provided by the Insight approach. This focuses the research questions on the parties' decisions to defend in response to feelings of threat.[23] When conflict dissipates, the research questions ask what occurred in the minds of parties so that threats no longer sustain the defence behaviour.

> The "Intransigent Conflict" is about an argument between me and my life partner over her use of cleaning products that I consider harmful. It is a case that exemplifies a spontaneous change of mind that is instigated through an altered space of encounter by the inclusion of a friend, whose casual remark evokes in me a fresh discernment of the significance of my partner's behaviour, which subsequently dissolves the argument and enduringly alters a pattern of interaction.[24]

Most compelling in her research is the way Jull demonstrates the relevance of attention to the mind's operations for the discipline of sociology.[25] The reflexive methodology of self-appropriation, as adapted for the discipline, provides access to important data about social change that is not otherwise available to researchers in the field. The case studies are filled with observations about her own operations of observing, understanding, verifying, feeling, valuing, deliberating, and deciding. Jull shows how the dynamics of change in the conflict cases are illuminated by the researcher's well-developed understanding and appropriation of her own mind's operations. What emerges is a portrait of conflict and change as arising from the interaction among parties' operations of meaning. The more insight we gain into the personal performance of these operations, it seems, the better we are able to understand the social dynamics of conflict and change.

For quality assurance, Jull combines the reflexivity methods drawn from the Insight approach with other tools drawn from sociology to cross-check, validate, and question the research results. The result is a significant expansion of the range of data available to the sociologist that is achieved without compromising the quality level of the research.

For learners in Insight studies, the book's four case studies offer compelling and engaging evidence that self-knowing is indeed worthwhile and can make a positive difference in personal life. Jull's own skills are impressive, and her ability to capture and communicate her performance in the written texts is remarkable. As a reader, I felt like I was observing the cases from the inside, not simply as a passing observer, but as an observer whose attention and insight are facilitated by a guide seasoned in the art of discernment. It would be difficult for me to imagine the experience of reading these chapters with no prior background in self-knowing. I get the impression, however, that Jull has managed to offer such readers an invitation and a fleeting glimpse: "Here's what it's like! Here's why it's worthwhile!" In this respect, I am not aware of another book quite like this one.

PSYCHOLOGY AND PROBLEM-SOLVING

Richard Grallo's book, *Question and Insight in Everyday Life,* arises from four decades of research and teaching in the field of applied psychology.[26] Through his career, he observed an "explosion" of publications on the topic of problem-solving.[27] The book offers what he judges to be a corrective to an important deficiency in this research, the absence of careful attention to central "mental events" as "facts of consciousness" that need to be observed and explained in their functional relationships if problem-solving is to be understood adequately. These facts of consciousness are "question," "insight," "the desire to know," and "social trust."

Readers familiar with the discipline of psychology will know that, as Grallo puts it, "mental events have a mixed reputation in well-established fields such as philosophy and psychology."[28] Instead of capitulating to this opinion or doing battle with his discipline, however, he calmly observes that the abundance of literature on the topic already gives the nod to specific facts of consciousness as important for understanding problem-solving. He takes this as validation of their significance for psychology and an invitation to carry forward a recognized research path. He notes that readers are indeed able to verify these facts of consciousness in their personal experience. And throughout the book, he appeals to a range of examples and illustrations to show how question, insight, the desire to know, and social trust arise frequently enough in everyday life to merit inclusion and be given priority in a more developed understanding of problem-solving.

In chapters 2 and 3, Grallo places his approach to problem-solving in dialogue with authors whose research focuses on critical thinking. And here we begin to understand why he claims that the research trajectory on problem-solving requires a corrective. He finds that approaches to problem-solving have been shaped significantly by research on critical thinking. After a background historical survey of this field, he finds a diversity of approaches that range from very wide definitions to very narrow definitions of critical thinking. Among the approaches that achieve greater precision, he finds that "The more narrow definitions focus on 'judgment' or 'decision' as a direct product of critical thinking."[29] His point, stated simply, is that if problem-solving involves the operations of experience, questioning, insight, judgment, and decision, then approaches that focus exclusively on only two of these mental events, judgment and decision, will yield overly narrow and skewed analyses. Moreover, if the full range of operations needs to be guided by the desire to know and social trust, then these, too, must play central roles alongside experience, question, insight, judgment, and decision in any adequate analysis of problem-solving. Thus, Grallo's book.

The core argument is developed in chapters 2 and 3. When the range of facts of consciousness is expanded, researchers are able to observe that the various mental events functionally interrelate in various patterns, and each pattern has its own distinctive guiding intention and endpoint or product.[30] Grallo lists four such patterns: he devotes chapter 2 to Pattern 1, and he devotes chapter 3 to Patterns 2, 3, and 4. Pattern 1, "Seeking Understanding," is the most important of the four because the guiding intention is shaped by the operations of question and insight, two operations typically neglected in other analyses. In addition, the inclusion of question and insight has the effect of altering the way the other three patterns are understood, even when they focus more directly on judgment and decision. This is because judgment and decision can no longer be understood purely logically; they must be understood as critical assessments of insights to determine whether they meet the criteria for passing specific tests.

> In Factual Critical Thinking (PS Pattern 2) the test is a test of truth or probability. In Values-oriented Critical Thinking (PS Pattern 3) the test is some standard of value or worth. In Deliberative Critical Thinking (PS Pattern 4) the test is a worthwhile course of action.[31]

The upshot is a rather detailed study of four patterns of problem-solving that can help readers work through problems methodically rather than haphazardly. The value-added lies in the self-control that readers can exercise when they learn to identify the facts of consciousness in themselves. To help in this learning, Grallo offers examples throughout the chapters, tables, and diagrams that organize insights for more visual learners, lists of points that help focus readers' attention, links with other literature in the field, and a chapter on "Examples of Facts of Consciousness in Other Perspectives" (chapter 6). The two other perspectives examined are those of Epictetus and Locke and Latham's "High Performance Cycle."

For college and university teachers, Grallo offers a textbook for an Insight studies course that can be used in a variety of disciplines. It is normal for various departments in post-secondary institutions to include courses on methodology and critical thinking in their programs, and instructors seeking novel approaches will find that Grallo widens the scope without sacrificing the rigour normally provided by narrower approaches. For human resource personnel in workplaces, Grallo offers a distinctive way of understanding "self-management" and a "learning personality." Employees need problem-solving skills to deal with challenges related to innovation, productivity, and workplace relationships. Grallo offers professionals a novel way of approaching problem-solving and thinking about the self-awareness component in workplace learning.

For all readers, Grallo offers a fascinating example of psychology done mindfully and self-reflectively. In his "Epilogue: Problem Solving as Mindful Practice," he summarizes the two ways his book aims to assist readers.

> First, it should facilitate attaining a special type of self-knowledge. This would be knowledge of the acts, operations, and processes involved in one's own problem solving efforts. Second, it should offer some guidance in self-management, allowing the reader to put this knowledge to use by better coordinating the mental events which enable human problem solving.[32]

The emphasis throughout is on "doing" the work involved in self-knowledge and self-management. Learners who have begun this path of practice in Insight studies will find that Grallo shows how applying self-knowing skills to the field of psychology can offer a fresh perspective that can entice and energize.

PHILOSOPHY AND SELF-POSSESSION

When I think back on my undergraduate courses in philosophy, nothing compares to Mark Morelli's book *Self-Possession: Being at Home in Conscious Performance*.[33] In my courses, I was instructed to read about others doing philosophy. Today, reading Morelli's book, I learn how to practise doing philosophy. If my mentors had followed the examples provided by music, chemistry, or hockey, the doing would have come first. At least, then, I would have known more about what I was reading. The book is clearly a course text in philosophy, and it points a way forward for readers interested in applying Insight studies skills to this discipline.

There is a lot going on in the book's fourteen chapters, but the overall project can be divided, roughly, into four sections. In the first section, including the "Prologue" and chapters 1–3, Morelli introduces readers to the practice of exploring our minds' operations and his own distinctive method using "meditations." I will say more about this method shortly. In the second section, chapters 4 and 5, he responds to philosophical questions about the curious meaning of the term "consciousness," and he invites readers into the task of ordering the operations into a framework he will use throughout the book. Along the way, he explores the role of "believing" in conscious performance and the cycles of progress and decline that can be observed in ourselves and our living.

In the third section, chapters 6–12, readers explore five different "motifs" that can be discerned in the ways the operations combine and play out in our lives. The fourth and final section reconnects readers with the analyses of sections 1 and 2. And here he invites us to observe how exploring conscious performance can carry us, not simply into self-knowledge, but towards a decision to take responsibility for acting on this knowledge in our daily living. The result of this decision and action is Self-Possession.

The third section is the longest, with fully half of the book's chapters, and it could be considered a journey of its own.[34] He takes readers into the self-discovery of five different "motifs" that arise in conscious performance, and he explains them in terms of the framework developed in chapter 5. We often observe that we use our minds to achieve practical tasks (motif 1). But sometimes we sit back and ask purely intellectual questions that are free from constraints imposed by immediate practicality (motif 2). At other times, our conscious engagement is artistic or aesthetic (motif 3). And quite often our conscious performance engages in navigating the challenges and achievements of interpersonal relations (motif 4). Finally, there is the motif of "mystical performance" (motif 5). What is striking is that each motif has its own distinctive "precepts" that can be observed in ordinary language in the various ways we use words like "should" and "ought."[35] Morelli seems to be saying that understanding the motifs could go a long way towards helping us deal with value conflicts we encounter in our relations with others. If he's right, and I suggest he is, learning the method could be quite important.

What sets Morelli apart from others is the method of using "meditations" to engage readers in the activity of doing the work of self-knowing.[36] The meditations are snippets from conversations we might have, either with others or with ourselves, using everyday language, raising questions and objections we would normally raise when faced with the author's statements and explanations. His method is to attend carefully to the language used in these snippets and to observe how the speaker invariably performs the very action she is challenging. It is this interactive way of engaging interlocutors in noticing the conscious performance operative in their questioning that is the key to the method. Here is a short section from an example he provides in the first chapter.

> When I make a commitment I usually know I'm making it ... But this basic commitment you're talking about seems to be one I may never have even thought about and don't remember ever making. Does it make sense to talk about having a commitment you don't even know you have and didn't ever make? Oh, wait a minute! Here I am trying to figure out why you're calling my interest in meaning, objectivity, knowledge, truth, reality, and value a basic commitment! So, in my trying to figure out why you're calling it a basic commitment I am actually illustrating the commitment you're talking about? I think I'm starting to get this now. It *is* strange.[37]

The book is filled with these meditations. A central feature is the way they display what Morelli calls "The Performative Self-Contradiction."[38] He calls it a "peculiar and troubling *contradiction between what we say and what we're doing when we say it.*"[39] We make a statement that affirms the objectivity of the truth that there are no objective truths. We make a statement that affirms the true value of rejecting true values. We claim to have objective knowledge of the fact that there is no objective knowledge.[40] By engaging readers in noticing these self-contradictions, Morelli directs attention away from the objects of our conscious operations and towards the operations themselves. In particular, he focuses attention on the inner normativity of the operations, a normativity that must be coherent with our thinking and acting.

Helping learners achieve this coherence is the aim of Morelli's project. His learning path focuses not simply on the life challenges that surround us, but on the life challenges that arise from within us. When we neglect the path of self-discovery, we live our lives in contradiction with ourselves, and these contradictions harm us and those around us. The meditations offer learners a method for discovering these contradictions, and this discovery reveals the first steps we can take along the road to Self-Possession. This, I would say, is worth pursuing.

POLITICS AND SPIRITUALITY

If Jull, Grallo, and Morelli offer rather curious ways of approaching the disciplines of sociology, psychology, and philosophy, Jamie Price's approach to politics in his book, *The Call*, will likely strike readers as the strangest of all.[41] The book is not simply strange in inviting readers to explore their minds' operations; it is strange in its style of presentation. The book unfolds as a dramatic dialogue between two figures, Sargent Shriver, founder of the Peace Corps, and Didymus, a fictional character Price has created so readers can experience Shriver speaking to them in his own voice. The reading experience is quite compelling.

Price is the founding director of the Sargent Shriver Peace Institute, and he spent much of his career as a university professor specializing in the works of Lonergan. Normally, we do not expect academic writers to serve up aesthetically engaging products, but every once in a while we are surprised. This book is one such surprise. Learners who have followed the path of Insight studies offered in these chapters know that self-appropriation can evoke the thrill of genuine wonder. When coupled with the aesthetic experience of Price's dramatic dialogue, this wonder is elevated to a new level. Who could imagine that reading in the field of politics could be as engaging as this?

The book arises from a twenty-year research project that produced a host of published materials.[42] But its signal products are two books: this one, authored by Price, *The Call: The Spiritual Realism of Sargent Shriver*; and a second, co-authored by the two of us, *Spiritualizing Politics without Politicizing Religion: The Example of Sargent Shriver*. The research presented in *Spiritualizing Politics* sets the background for *The Call*. And that context is the troubling task of navigating the distinctions and relations between religion and politics in order to bring life-giving resources from religious traditions into political programs in the service of peace at home and abroad. The goal of the project is to find a way of rising above the bitter effects of conservative-liberal and religious-secular divisions. The chosen strategy is to explore the words and deeds of a major American political figure, Robert Sargent Shriver.

Shriver offers an example of a public figure whose Catholic faith influenced the development of American political programs that are still recognized as important today. He was a leading figure in the Catholic Interracial Council movement in the United States. He was the founding director of the Peace Corps under President Kennedy. He developed America's War on Poverty under President Johnson. And, in partnership with his wife, Eunice Kennedy Shriver, he was chairman of Special Olympics International.[43]

A recurring theme throughout the speeches of Shriver's public life is this: "Politics needs religion to do its work."[44] A central religious influence needed by politics, for Shriver, is the transformative gift of the spirit as operative in the lives of citizens. The key word here is gift. The result of this gift in us is something that previously would have been beyond us: a dedication to the service of others. Shriver lived out this dedication to service personally, and he built it into the organizational fabric of the Peace Corps.

Price uses the language of spirituality to explore this dedication to service in the politics of peacebuilding. What is most interesting about *The Call*, however, is the way he uses the method of self-knowing to invite readers into discovering the spirit in their own selves. Through the dialogue between Shriver and Didymus, readers are drawn into the method of attending to their own minds. In "Conversation 3, Catcher," for example, Shriver invites Didymus into a roleplay situated in a baseball game.

> RSS: Right now. Imagine you're in the role of a ballplayer coming up to bat in a ballgame. I'll be the catcher.
> DYD: You want me to imagine myself in the batter's box?
> RSS: That's right. Take on the role.
> DYD: Okay. I'm stepping up to the plate, getting into my stance.
> RSS: Good. Notice that as you take on that role, the horizon of what you're wondering about tracks with it.
> DYD: What should I be noticing?
> RSS: Just pay attention to where your mind takes you in your role. What are you wondering about? What are you concerned about?[45]

Eventually, through a series of such self-investigations, Shriver helps Didymus discover that he is able to notice, not simply the events of an experience in political life, not simply his conscious mind engaging with these events, but also the presence of the spirit as operative in his consciousness, tugging him towards self-transcendence.[46] Through the chapters, the characters develop a model for differentiating the presence of the spirit.[47] And readers observe Didymus struggling with the model in a way that draws them into the dialogue and into the self-appropriation process.

In the final chapter, "Conversation 9, Peace Corps: Blessed Are the Peacemakers," Price provides a portrait of events leading up to the event of the book's title, the phone call from President Kennedy inviting Shriver to take the lead in designing and launching the Peace Corps. Prior to the election, during Kennedy's campaign, public interest in the Peace Corps arose in a way that Shriver likened to a "spontaneous combustion."[48] At the centre of this surge of public support were the responses of more than a thousand students to a letter published in *The Michigan Daily* by Judith and Alan Guskin. In taking Didymus through a roleplay that situates him in the middle of these events, Shriver mentors Didymus in the practice of following the model and discerning the spirit operative in his own response to the call to self-transcending service.[49] The dramatic dialogue provides readers with powerful resources for engaging in the same process of spiritual self-discovery that is modelled by the characters.

While the book's title suggests the focus on Peace Corps, Price also explores Shriver's response to the call to service in combatting racism in Chicago during the 1950s.[50] For Shriver, peacebuilding was not simply a work we do abroad. Rather, in the early years of his public life in Chicago and in his later years after his tenure as director of the Peace Corps, Shriver's call was to service at home, responding to the challenges of racism and poverty. Through the chapters, Price takes Didymus and his readers through the events of Shriver's public life in the 1950s with the Catholic Interracial Council of Chicago, working to racially desegregate Catholic schools. As in the Peace Corps chapters, his focus is always on readers, inviting them into the self-knowing process, attending to the operation of the spirit tugging them towards their own best selves. Notice that Price's argument is not that we *ought* to do something to bring the spirit into our lives in politics. Rather, with Shriver, he is convinced the spirit is already working in all of us.[51] Our task is to discern this operation and cooperate with it. This, I suggest, adds a novel and interesting dimension to the discipline of politics.

CONCLUDING REFLECTIONS

The six authors surveyed here offer readers avenues for advancing and applying their Insight studies skills to the disciplines of ethics, conflict studies, sociology, psychology, philosophy, and politics. To be sure, the works of these authors will be of interest to students pursuing studies in these fields. But they will also be of interest to scholars and researchers working in the fields. The skills of Insight studies introduce a level of self-awareness into the horizon of researchers, and this expands the range of data relevant to the enquiry. The six authors surveyed here offer glimpses of how this self-awareness and data can change the direction of work in the various fields.

Another benefit arising from the six authors' works is the contribution each offers to life skill development. In each case, the author signals avenues for building on the basic skills learned in these modules. Their works help readers discern directions whose pursuit can help learners wrestle with challenges in the home, in relationships, in workplaces, and in the activities of social and political life. Through the course of our lives, we frequently wrestle with serious ethical issues, conflicts that threaten our relationships, arguments that tear us apart, problems we need to solve, questions about the worth of living, and challenges that threaten the fabric of social and political order. There is a component of self-knowledge and critical thinking that needs to be developed in order to discern and live out our responsibilities as partners, parents, neighbours, workers, and citizens. The skills of Insight studies set learners on a road towards developing this self-knowledge and critical thinking. And the authors surveyed here offer indications of paths of development that lie ahead for serious learners.

CHAPTER SIX

Afterword

Insight studies is a practice-based approach to self-knowledge and critical thinking. The approach followed in the modules of these chapters offers learners a step-by-step method for working with puzzles. The method is patterned after the way we learn to play musical instruments: daily practice and detailed exercises that focus on building skills from the ground up. The skills that learners develop in the modules are the skills required for observing, understanding, verifying, and taking responsibility for the operations of our minds. These are the operations we use in the normal activities of day-to-day living, learning, and problem-solving. When these skills are developed, learners find they can be helpful in situations requiring the specialized use of our minds' operations, situations where scholars and researchers are charged with developing and verifying explanatory theories that meet challenges that affect large numbers of people over long periods of time.

The importance of Insight studies for various disciplines is highlighted in the works of the six authors surveyed in chapter 5. They all address an interesting fact that tends to get overlooked in their disciplines. This fact is that knowledge, when affirmed by a specialist in a field, is always the result of her performance of her mind's operations. Disciplines train specialists to focus on the objects of these operations. But the reliability of results depends on the specialist's competent performance of the operations themselves. To ensure competent performance, specialists need skills for attending carefully to the operations so they can be assured they are performing them properly. Training in these skills, however, seldom forms part of the education of specialists. Insight studies offers a corrective for this oversight.

We have arrived at a moment in history when citizens in democracies seem to have lost confidence in knowledge. We are confused about knowledge and about how we are to deal with conflicting claims to knowledge on important issues. Social media has raised the impact of this problem to the level of a crisis. But social media is not the source of the problem. Rather, the source of the problem is the oversight. The disciplines responsible for knowledge will help in navigating these challenges to the extent that they take up the invitation offered by the six authors surveyed here. Fortunately, as citizens, we need not wait for the experts to launch our own programs for self-knowing and critical thinking.

There is a reason why the learning path offered here has been neglected. Our minds have a normal, default orientation that focuses attention on the objects of our minds' operations: the things we see and hear, the things we understand, the things we verify, and the courses of action that we and others decide and actuate. As we perform these various operations, the operations themselves are also present to us in ways we can observe. If we are trying to figure out the answer to a question, if asked what we are doing, we can notice that we are attending to data, we are asking a question, and we have not yet discovered the answer. But noticing something occasionally is quite different from investigating something methodically. To investigate our minds' operations methodically requires that we stretch our minds. This takes practice.

When we first stretch our minds to focus on the operation of insight, for example, we can sometimes notice the sudden experience of an insight. However, if we do, our minds snap back to their normal, default orientation immediately afterwards. If asked to talk about the insight, we invariably talk about the object of the insight, the thing we understood. We have not noticed that we have shifted back to our default orientation. To gain an accurate understanding of the operation requires that we shift our attention away from the object and fix it firmly on the operation each time it occurs. It requires examining insights time after time and attending carefully to the before-and-after transformation that occurs. This requires stretching our minds so that they do not snap back to their default orientation. Like our muscles, stretching our minds to do new things requires daily practice. When we do this, however, a wonder-filled world of new data becomes present to us.

Insight studies offers learners access to this wonder-filled world of new data. It offers colleges and universities opportunities to expand the horizons of both students and researchers. And these expanded horizons will prove helpful in meeting the social and political challenges of our time. I suggest that Insight studies will be of special interest to colleges and universities whose heritage and mission are rooted in religious traditions.[1] This is because Insight studies offers ways of bringing resources from religious traditions to learners from all traditions through the method of self-discovery. As Price has shown, these resources include the self-discovery of a spiritual dimension of our conscious selves, a dimension that is at work in us, calling us to be our best selves.

Most important is the impact Insight studies can have in disciplines like psychology, sociology, conflict studies, and political science. As Jull has shown, the focus on "reflexivity" has become thematic in sociology, and the self-reflective attention of researchers has become common enough to warrant attention. Insight studies offers a method for bringing this self-reflective attention to full fruition in ways that can impact this and other fields. As Grallo has shown, attention to the operations of questioning, insight, the desire to know, and social trust changes the way we understand problem-solving. And as Picard has shown, attention to the operations of questioning, insight, judgment, and bias can transform our understanding of the roots of conflict and avenues for resolution. These impacts are not minor; they are major. They can become a learning institution's way of shaping its disciplines in novel ways that are both faithful and intellectually sound.

One final note. The impact of Insight studies will be far-reaching. This is because it offers a new way of answering the question: What kind of organism am I? The answer we discover in practising the modules is that I am a knower, and I can learn about my operations of knowing. I can gain self-knowledge and learn to think more critically, more responsibly. At first, this does not seem like much. But eventually we discover that learning lies at the heart of everything we do. It is what nourishes our relationships. It is what resolves conflicts. It is what solves problems. It is the central work of parenting. It lies at the centre of all our commercial transactions. It is what transforms us from apathy or intransigence to open engagement. It is the heart of innovation, both material and social. It is the work of managers forever charged with leading teams. It is the path we follow in ethical discernment. It is the resource we engage when mobilizing the spirit in political action. It is what we are built to be and become.

The time has come to understand that self-knowledge and critical thinking cannot be achieved simply by reading books or listening to lectures. Something else must accompany the readings and lectures if the relevant meanings are to be understood correctly. This something else is regular practice in a program of self-reflective skill development. Self-knowing is not just gathering information. It requires skill development, like playing the violin. This takes time and effort, but everything worthwhile takes time and effort, and this is worthwhile. These modules have been developed for learners and mentors who take innovation seriously and are willing to try something new, something that, at first, seems strange and awkward. Even Lonergan scholars, I expect, will find the approach odd. I offer these modules in the hope that a practice-based approach to self-knowledge and critical thinking becomes a topic in various departments of the colleges and universities responsible for learning. I think this is a good time for the practice-based methods of Insight studies.

APPENDIX

Scramble Words

Four Letters

YDDE	AGLL	EAHC	DJAE	ALIR
EOZN	OILD	APML	ZORE	CLAK
NEPA	ADNH	ITAW	CTAT	YORU
AEMS	AZEL	AEKM	GASG	AHSM
ISDK	EABL	CRAE	WFIA	RASE
IPDA	NHCI	LSDA	DSMA	ATKL
MAMI	SDOE	OZMO	ASLP	IFRA
AGGO	ENAJ	MNAE	ENTA	FTAR
DEMA	ASNF	JASB	PTEK	TUNO
MDPA	LASB	CENA	TIED	KCEA
EMDA	NEAD	AJZZ	IBSI	KASY
APRI	PEGA	ADER	EEAS	OYAG
LCAT	LUEY	FAÉC	OYEB	OOEB
GERO	AMNI	DONW	BSGA	RKCA
IALN	NUSR	TGEA	RASO	UGYL
AELV	EASL	EATL	EAWK	LATH
LFAC	AKRD	UNOP	GRSA	BAYB
NYAK	LBEA	RSUE	CBAK	ALEM
KTEA	KEAF	CAEM	FAEC	ERTF
ABTE	KPEE	VYAN	IMDA	ZTSE
MAAM	RSAJ	DPAS	ABKL	HELA
NAPI	ADIC	AMLC	LHFA	BAEB
SMIP	GSAA	JBMA	UEGR	DMAE
KEAL	ALLW	CHOE	NSPA	SYEA
WAED	ILAM	LKPE	JSMA	OAHL
YJSA	MIGA	PEYL	ISLA	DASD
ADEG	ILAP	PAEC	SEKY	FEDA
GWAS	AKSC	ALLB	ARDI	REAL
KACL	LDAE	RENA	SDIA	GGAE
MEGA	EELK	HAKC	FATD	LAGI
PSIZ	KSGE	INTU	PTCA	FAFG
TASB	IBTA	AENC	KADN	CNIA
UGRB	CAKJ	IKKC	ALLT	KEAS
SEGA	TOAS	LAFL	DSDO	LSLI
DFAS	EKCN	OASK	IELD	IAED
ESSU	FLIA	LEAG	BLIA	AFEM
IUTQ	CASB	RYCA	CATF	AWKL
QUDA	GNIA	YDRA	ASTL	LDAB
WYLA	AALM	OHTA	OEKY	YNRA
OICN	ENRA	CAKP	VNEA	GLSA
CAKT	AVNI	ACLL	TLIA	FAES

Five Letters

IMPYL	KERSA	BSAUE	MSNEA	ELFTI
AIENN	AQTRU	EESPH	LADTE	ATHRE
SAPRH	KOCSO	SEESK	FAEBL	APECE
ELAPR	ABEAT	NSSTE	THHCI	ISEZE
OEOZS	FFHTI	DENSE	KAKCN	LSKTI
SOEMO	IRQKU	EROAP	BALBE	BGNIE
DBEGA	ONCUT	AOEVB	JATUN	SECTA
OERGG	ASLML	EKMRA	HFTIG	IETRN
LAMSP	LTYLA	SOGEO	ESTHE	OTGSH
NKOKC	ALPLE	TAOBO	EETCR	RNDIK
CSFEA	BDRIA	REYNT	UCHNH	RRBYE
CELSA	EAPDL	RACSE	SELEA	QITEU
ANDKR	SESAM	KRSAC	NASYT	VSPEA
ASRIE	CRREA	EHSOL	NLECA	UHTHC
ICJEU	HATHC	DLSAN	GTOAN	EERNV
QLUEA	AODRI	HRSAK	ROTWH	FKENI
HRYRU	OESNP	ECBNH	KNSEC	ILNFA
ESSDE	RITDH	GESNU	SAEYS	ALQIU
BACNO	HAROB	ANFKR	OFFRE	ULQIT
UGJDE	ORKJE	ESSDK	RYELA	MAISL
GAEDR	DAEBI	VIOEL	AIMNA	BECSU
NIJTO	IMEAG	UNRDE	BYAEB	CUNMI
EENVR	EMSAK	CHATR	RMFAE	FYFTI
PDTOE	NLMYA	TAITN	UCIRN	TRIKC
TCLHA	MNOGA	TDHEP	PCNAE	GLTHI
UKIQC	CPHEA	KISCK	FGSTI	PSSTE
RTGAE	AELBL	RAIBB	OVEYN	GNWSI
YSASB	HAHRS	ABBTO	AWSLH	RHABS
JMROA	NJSOI	LTPSE	ROERR	ISEUS
ADRRA	OSRCK	FJYFI	OROUD	OITPC
ACESH	TONEF	PAEUS	BTOAU	AIALV
EARHT	EEGNR	DGSOO	LPESA	UNNIO
PLIEM	KAPSE	GDBEA	NKSKI	CSLUO
RISLA	QUAML	DEMNO	LASKE	MODLA
ENHYO	LBYAD	GCMIA	CHNEI	DNEGU
JUTSO	MIHDU	TTKYI	TIGNH	ROTVE
NEIFR	KINSG	HEYTM	JENYN	SEPSR
PITNE	DAEKR	MSIOT	DEELV	OHURG
BRDYE	SEQTU	AGLRE	EORLD	SAKRP
MSLBA	CTTIA	VNLAA	LYJLE	WESET
CAYRR	ACTHE	CUHCO	CSBKA	EATTR
PAWSN	OCRCU	MAMDA	GIATN	HSEUR
HCTIK	FALIR	ENLSA	NASIL	EVIOC
QUKAC	EAEGL	GOITN	FAITN	TIRWE

Appendix   111

Six Letters

AIRUSD	HBTLOC	CSLEUN	TRTEJI	LSAVEU
RWBROO	GYAVEO	RTIALA	RTHNOE	IPEMDE
KEREEP	RRTATA	KELREN	LGGGEI	ARPEDI
ELCDTU	ADECRA	REAIRV	EJGANL	ILAICT
EXPFRI	AACRIB	ICTTCA	ATTERS	MROUAR
EGENNI	EPPCRO	REFWSA	AROTRO	LNOCUI
CLNKIE	VSLIAU	YCVONO	TVAACN	RODRBE
LTTKEE	RPDONE	RAHTLE	IRDEGL	IRATOL
ERNAOG	RAHTFE	UAQOEP	RRALEG	NLEEED
SRYLAA	NLISEA	ENGGRI	NLTUGE	OLLHWO
UEOPCN	FICORL	GTSAIN	NLDAVA	LBBREA
ETTPRO	LBBHEO	RYPERA	TTLABE	SQLUIT
ITCACR	OEHSTN	TGANEE	NRRGAE	GOIGLO
AKWERL	LESDAI	SASPKR	DLIARA	DRDEKI
ULRANE	FASUEN	ARMTCA	ILRASP	MGERIA
OFEFCI	HNEALD	LKNENE	LGGBEO	VEXROT
TNUSIL	TUNJYA	RFTALE	ELPDXU	RLDADE
UYITEQ	VESEER	LCCAIT	EABRAL	NEINTT
MNTIEU	URENET	DAGGRE	PNOOHC	SDEALD
AICRLA	RNTECA	NEUNDB	NMIFEA	HKUONO
NYASTI	SFELIT	IBBBNO	GRDGIE	RIFFDE
NEKDIL	NKIUDN	PASSHL	MARADA	NLAIDS
EICSSP	ENISTP	EOPCRO	OGTHET	AELSTT
LRTKAE	JCTAEK	DEHRCN	TLECAK	TRERAS
WRDEPO	LMVLEU	LSGSYO	TNEALG	TAELTN
SLIVEA	SYIMAL	AECLOR	EGRTTA	ROPPHE
SREJET	FLWAOL	LPMSEA	PGOCNI	MYELHO
PIOONT	PEPOSO	EASMES	TALLWE	PSIECO
GSIENN	RNATAT	BTGLOE	RTKANE	OKJEYC
TIOMPR	UPEMRI	CNLOUS	QOMUUR	RHDINE
CEEASP	PERROT	EETTSL	VUMCAU	SEIUNR
NDDEBO	YIECNT	AONRCE	NTEARU	SVCOIE
NMELTA	RRAFEM	ITPSIR	UOMFSA	CTAREK
TMFHAO	ACTUML	PURNWA	ESTPRO	YONHJN
DRAREN	OATTTO	BEROLW	RRVESE	FLYMAI
ESEPHR	SRTEMI	TOSFFE	IRTEWA	LBBKEI
LESIPC	ISEPMO	SRUDET	ONBETN	NEONJI
GYREES	BOYLDO	MEOHGA	ESRJYE	YAINVT
VLJIOA	USEENA	ESSTLA	TFFRAI	IFSMTI
DNMEOR	VNTEAR	SRTEFA	LTTNEE	KGINTA
IROBEL	RIENEM	ATFENS	RSLAIO	TRLTAE
IBNLEB	PINDKA	RRFEPE	ITMENT	DSYORW
SNXHPI	CSTIEH	HERTIH	INKEYD	RUANDO
RITBAB	UEQETA	IEDSTG	CEROOL	GEIWLG

Appendix

Seven Letters

DTEIOIN	ODYOOHB	OTNURCN	IAALNLV	ADRLSDE
ENSERTW	CISMIVT	TNOYEHS	RADMEER	FHSERIS
NCUEKIQ	OIZSMEB	TAATTCR	NNETILE	EECURTL
CASTCRH	UISREMP	AIRATDE	LPSTHAA	TERIPLX
UACDETE	ORBSCUE	LEEREPS	EENWGPI	JGRLEUG
YTIROSH	OSLARLD	IRTINMP	ILLKSET	BJTOSEC
ELASUOZ	ETXERUT	WLISLPO	APMTRAR	AIEPRNT
EFLERAW	WLYDLOR	BOOURBN	RVBADAO	CELPSIE
RRALEWC	HRINSVA	GALACIL	LTEREOC	AKUWLEF
ABIVTER	MFAGNIY	PCEACOK	RZIOHON	DWGINRA
AATULSS	TCACTIS	OILGAND	HSYICSP	WNELDIG
SNIEEFS	LEDYLRE	ARSETNE	IKCRCET	ORSOUNE
FOACTIN	EEARTHN	IEJSTRT	EENKGPI	YPAERML
RCREKAC	SISIKNG	ANOJRIT	PISLEAC	TASNTEN
ETGECLN	IDNREDK	HTTEERA	ROREPOT	TIMETIA
LHNTEIG	AHRISNT	SEKNCAA	RPWPEAR	NAATURL
OOHERNM	ENNIOTM	WWDARAY	EARPOTE	SOAUNTD
ETWHEAR	ITFRDER	QEUILFY	KLENNES	OERRACT
RNIREKD	RITTYNI	ABATULE	PNOINEG	WNAITIG
OLDONES	CLOURTY	UISLACM	OEHFUPL	DIDEWNG
OGLINDH	SGETHIW	RKSETAC	CASITIA	NOUUTCH
RECYNSE	UKCSELB	IGNINDF	NPIUJER	EUOYRJN
NVALAEC	IZDOLIE	ETRNIIA	OLUNARJ	NROGKWI
UACDSRT	YTIRAED	RMCATEE	NEINSCE	OENEWRH
GLANIIF	NSEOINP	LLLGAEI	IBNAROW	PNSETLA
NAEHTRU	OYCETIS	UTSECIJ	ELRESVO	UAMGSNT
HPYILAP	NREATIT	INICEKT	RIRETER	VIISOER
KSPHIIN	RLOSAEC	REPEEDC	UNMSIOB	AGTVNAR
ILONPDH	OLUHSAG	GENLIOB	RTLETIG	RRUKECT
RBAELRW	UTJIFSY	OWEBSTI	QEUARRL	IETLARL
ABAHTIT	BLBUBES	STEELTK	UGNOYER	OIPTILC
RKGEALC	SVELESS	ACNMEHI	PISHASN	UAEQRRT
OERNGIF	RCOROTP	EIUTNQT	MIRTOON	EMTITRE
ENYOMCO	AKRPSER	UDESITO	JUEALOS	IGSDSRE
DAIGITL	PGUTRHI	SBEREMM	OATELBN	RTDCVIE
SUEBLOL	NTKRIET	EARNCBK	IHEEVLC	APNNSKI
UMRRSOU	GVAIREN	CARMERE	FRFCEIO	PAEREKS
EOGLBNI	RNUNNIG	ETARCWH	ORSOWRS	SENEEZS
OLGIKDE	ELORDSI	UDBRIEL	UTATERQ	HLWREEE
INNGGSE	TGANENT	OUECTPL	SDAELDS	ICOFNTI
UNILDMF	ISFIOSN	LGIYHNT	ELCDUCO	UFMLEFR
LUKELUE	SSCYTEA	LEOULBG	AISCETC	SDEELEN
TIRSADE	OPSECIH	TCOTOYB	IOCNURN	ATRANRW
RECOFPS	GWNNIOS	NGISTHK	SNUREDA	MULSEGG

Eight Letters

VECSGEAN	MAITIEST	RAWMETOK	WOLAYRNR
AMGNATSE	EPOETYNH	ACNROOSC	NLMAIFET
ENMRSUTI	EEAERBGV	HNIMPCOA	PSELDAOR
RAIDTACM	IIDENYFT	NOAILADG	SVLIEDIH
LNANIPCE	AORHYRNO	NMNAMIET	ILDIFTYE
LGAUNTET	ACEMRELK	HSRAEICV	OTPAEMHR
NLANDSGI	ERMAMNEB	NUCNENAO	LVNEUJIE
LITAANEE	CPOIOSLC	ECHAMSRB	RYUGTAAN
IREUPSTC	EHNMHANC	OOTBLEES	ATLTSESI
NYOBRDUA	TMAGNCIE	APTCICYA	GGLIEYRN
EENTTMNE	WOEBRORR	PNPDAIXE	RINDIPGP
ESOHSLPE	ALIHNACP	MOLAYNRD	TCEBDJOE
RICTAEHT	FFVEISEU	IALKAENL	AOICLTCK
SKENSDWE	TNARCCIO	HIECCALM	KRGAISNN
IMAILRPE	LGOAETEN	EELTSATC	YMLPORAO
IMLAFDON	EINKSHTC	ENAILNGR	IANYTIFL
ACNTILGK	INZFILEA	IMNIBALO	OEVRONGR
RRPOOAET	AGLFNTOI	IDNONTAM	VEOLARTE
OCLSDFAF	FDREALUD	TIEMRSNI	RPEDIEEG
IBENESTF	EOEMDOTR	RCETIIRF	IFNENEIM
LBZEMEZE	OGTAENIN	RENEZGEI	ANOTHHRW
GLNAHGIU	ARTGEUAD	ILNPGKAN	INNOGMCO
CCRHKSEE	EEIGHNET	ETACTSSL	ILASISDY
LCASDRPA	ENIOTDOV	OATNTEAN	IHGSSEHN
ELLBTTEI	IJAVESNL	INAILEBN	TNUAISLU
NDFEERIE	MUMYTIIN	TRDEEHIY	IOLMARKG
PRPLAVAO	ESAORRBB	INUEMRGA	EEIKNPFN
AEIRLCCL	CSNKEKUL	DYOOLIGE	PEIMCLSA
IILTNAMT	IUSAHNLG	URKAEDCH	ADOLRRAI
UIOLSNIL	OLNEGAHD	TEIHCOPN	DESIILMA
EYULOJSA	LIOOGUSR	EOCNTICT	ETOCNRHE
RTOLNEEC	LOWDOGIL	ANPLSTII	ILNFGTEE
AEAGULGN	ELREYWJE	OENNSRUT	IFAMISEL
ARNGTNIO	MOPMUIER	EHRESAFT	ISLSNIOK
MSAANLTI	ANMHOSED	ANCEHOCR	ORMIOSPT
BENOEITD	LNICTEOE	ARADISLC	TAKNLBES
ARNTEFES	ACSPIFMI	LENIAACL	AMEJROEB
BITNOEDA	ADKLILEY	SPARPAIE	HEELNTNG
LZIDRABZ	UISCJEST	EAGYTILL	GHOEEGHD
IJAUCLID	LTNAWDII	DETONATE	RAIANNMD
ABSIMTIG	ESOERGUN	BNIIVOOL	ELEENSSD
NHARMCIO	AYIORMTJ	ROBSCSEU	ASTRANER
OLAECSCE	ASNGELEO	OTNIDONA	RAHTELES

Nine Letters

ASIOIRHLU	SGIPNNOOI	TTAESSAUR	TNAADREIM
RWMECAOIV	ISTESUQEN	AGNSEALGU	ACRBOESHL
BFTOASEUC	MSRIUASME	PLOLHYUEF	RYTNELLAE
ERUFOCSOI	EATRRDWHA	AAERCTLSO	COPENEDIT
MELIOANRZ	AAPSUPATR	ITMEQPEUN	ACADEVETU
IDMLEAANT	DTOPSNENI	RRPAEIPAS	AITEERGMH
VOCANDEIA	JEEWRYLLE	DRAPNEPAS	LCEIAITSR
GLCALYAIL	NDPPIAKDE	ALOSLOPLH	PECALEAEB
TRYASEDNB	FTEEDDSRO	NRATAWRIE	AILPLFYNU
QUSENSITO	TEMODUATA	TFFGNUBIE	GYRCLAOIH
ELMNAIURC	CKBOHKCEO	ITECFNEID	DYAESIHAW
LTIILLOVM	NSHTEEPUO	DIGHLNFOC	TETNOEDIN
NYLEARATP	HERIUOATZ	REMOPSIVI	MEABLMFAL
ANRMOAYDT	ATSISNALA	NKIEMSIIB	IEESGRGNT
KSUPARBNT	RQUUBESLE	ODATERDCE	CERILEGYN
NSNEHIPOS	KICIRTEPN	IOSNGCNLE	OTITPARMN
NRFSENIGI	NDEERSAEG	CEUFTULTA	SEUHTMOEA
OLBETDAAP	SWEEEDETN	LPIUTTOOA	HETAOFRPO
IESLCTALO	OPIHSANMC	EREDRVOAH	BFSMELIEI
UALQRTYRE	CSHKIAEPC	DYRUALLAG	MAINEDUCR
ESOLVEITN	FECSNFOER	IADSDTCEE	RSNSUHIOE
ENOGMWORH	RTIRCYICU	RCARTTATO	RFHCSEKEI
TWUTOHOGR	OILOFNTTA	AEMUYPCRS	OEXSNHAPO
DEDASTILE	NFEOORVPO	BRBMRIAAS	ATIEMTIPN
PRREOUSEH	EOSGIOTLG	LGFINTNAI	GSNBWLUAO
ATOSLOFLB	LZAKEABIN	BNATLHIYR	NKLTICOLF
ECNNIAETR	ASSNEIMPH	RENOEOMTM	AYEJKARWL
TEFDANTLE	MSCYETIHR	ARADIINWN	GBPKGAYIC
MENISONTA	MIUNNGRBE	CETRLYIAN	EADHNWSDI
UILSPMLRA	HSTTESIIC	BAKCPTWSE	THIETSINK
IYRGTIFAN	YETCPCISA	INCAGLNAB	NNSIGIFIH
ERTSTUNNI	WOASLDYRP	OZABELGIL	FEDUSMLAI
ANPRAREIM	TSRLAYSLE	GNTADEMER	CINNIGDLU
INATGMIIT	EETDSORMO	RYAUSNDKJ	AVRENSISO
NRAGENCOI	IIMETUHAL	ETADECSRT	GINLYALRG
AEARRHCTC	AKSUDINCQ	YEHDTREDA	NLPHSERIE
CERIEASMK	VEAGTTRIA	LASRIKMAE	AIORGZNRE
IDOIICAMT	AORSGEIND	BTAEEBLAD	ELSCOUELL
DIKTNELIS	CHHETIHIK	QEIETETUT	OBESNTVRA
NESWERAPP	WSAKRLCOS	AGSEERSEN	NRIISGEUF

Ten Letters

NEGRIETHNA	TVREERTXSO	ENLOIGSDRM	EORGRPNMFI
ANMAKSREIR	ENWNDISASR	INNNIOAGTM	UOMDSCEITZ
FEOSDTEEDR	OMDLNZAEEB	TRICAAOYNU	GAUTFIVIER
RUANAGOTDI	TGPOUEIDSS	LILSAROTCO	HNARSEDABL
RCBIHDEESI	YANSSBRDTE	NUYITALJLB	ZISERMDMEE
IHHRTHEICK	JOEZERPIDA	AANEELMLBT	REBIISFCRK
IOINPKTFNE	LUDTIPIMEL	RCMAEPEDAS	ELTONRGDAE
AYALOFTMNB	UZDLSRLBEO	UCENKARTCR	HEFPDAIRNT
NERIASHTBE	LRISOFESUH	RSMREDEASK	IAETPCIPLR
MVATBANLIE	OSWERYNTWH	TUIFOITSIC	AUURIATNEG
OECEPCSTIL	ATHCKCTMIS	TCSIIIVAET	ALEHNTSIOS
ELLHNRCGAE	EFRARTUSDT	ROURTDSGES	GEHHNETDEI
LDAAIDVSNE	ETSELRBLSE	OASSLRECES	LNFGEIRDIR
MAEBTLEIST	ONRDIEAGTC	SNALARTUTI	CRAETNDITO
OLRABFDYAF	NRIEVILAAB	APNCICOPCU	IIPWSTEVNO
CBSTRMOOKI	IDLINSKENS	RUOUTANOBD	HNAEINNGTC
GSRSAIOGNE	YTLMLCYSAI	ANEPLIRILK	UDSRERSDLE
EELRVTIARN	AKNBIIGCRF	EILESUBROL	EALTYISICT
ROEOIPSNSP	NERXAYELTL	ETIEGNLAOB	DERRNOURNA
NTMIYLTIEA	ITILAAGENN	ECDIROOCSL	NATLCIZEER
WGNSIEGARG	DTERPIAENS	EUEPETRPAT	TMEEIARIVP
RPEEMTPIPN	NIOLLAAACG	VCODEOEART	NAPHNOGLEO
OOHLLMAICS	UMIFTNLFEL	VUHRDEEOLA	EOORVWERDK
SOSEHUBRES	OIEXTESMNP	IHISUNMACT	REDTBEHFEA
EPIOETTIDN	BNANTHIEMS	ONOESRMHEW	ALROADUNTM
TEAJSUPSOX	EANLCMAIHC	ALNIRHDTNE	OECNTFAORN
MTUONAIITL	VAILRISEET	OEATSMTINI	ADKGINERLE
OLSIBMSEIP	NPDNDAHOEE	FRAESOMSUH	EDALOFWNNL
IKTERNGWNO	IASTOLABNT	AKIJBATCBR	SEYLISADFC
NITWNRTEEI	DAEIPRLHSE	TAFICBDUER	ATKEAQERUH
TARILCDCEU	GTAGSRHNIE	YABRKDEERO	RORTNEHNER
ERIYTVRNEA	ELOEARTCLA	UNLSRENGGI	OABELMMITS
PRAODTEOHN	AATTCHRLIE	VAGRSEEEDL	BAREIVEILF
NTOLEEIBAC	EVTAYTGNII	IMMTYUAIRT	DAIITICESL
CRANGAEIKT	INGAOLLRYI	ACCEDDRTIE	AELDIESRVD
ITREPPECVE	SSUUSCPOII	SOSNMARIYI	LVOUIURTYS
IESNGINLGT	LRTAEPCEEC	GCHLNUBIST	UMLLAERVSO
ALZABREODR	UATBIEINCA	AREFTCDBAI	OTRMAOBSOT
BELOBVESAR	ARAYBLRTOO	SEYEIORGTN	XLLYCECEEN
ETTUTOSFRI	UAITDELCTV	NIECBIAELF	BTCANNESEI

Eleven Letters

UQVRSCEIKLI	ABEJKESWRRA	GAIUNPLDTIC	SFILNITFAOC
PANMTICDEEA	EHLTAIYCLNC	NAIGAALERIT	OUKCNHSNIRG
OIDBNBNKIOG	OJSSARTLNIU	RERHEEECADL	CTONHMOTOTU
NINENSOIIVG	IETACNNANUS	UOIRBIETTRN	YLNAIRTILLB
LWLFERAOKOR	IAMCNSOSGTI	ERDELICRIBU	NELUNPAPIAG
SUTILCITAEA	RISOZUTREMI	YOARGIMPLOT	TMSEHITSEHC
SYROETOMCLC	LAMMAITRGCA	MODOARTLBES	ECQAELEUVIN
NIYREEMLVAD	TSMEREEAUNM	CSTEIIRNORT	IIYSNLFPIMG
SNHIGFTOLPI	NTOWEEMNLAG	REKHBTEOARN	RHLAWIKGTEN
FAUELITYLBU	ILEOINMSEST	AMLYRTLFEUS	LITDIUENMAL
EOIMEBLAZTS	CIAIITURSTL	SCORRTEIMEM	TTOPIEMTSOR
GETPNLASRIT	BTVOSCIEIJT	IMERNAIZITU	MAENURALPIT
NCNOOTIERID	ORAFITUNNCY	STTIVEISIEF	SPYSITNLOLE
NLBKLKECAUL	UBTRILEGFHL	SPCNETIAATI	YEAITSLSNLE
OLSMRTOUNSY	DNIIYIGENTF	DTIANUTLALI	IALTICIGNIZ
KRIISSHNFGE	EOTSNPINMRE	HPEPTMSOCIR	AEKWBEASSTT
PEHSROPIOLH	ANDIICIEVVT	YECCASSBERP	YHIGNHNAETP
IVNEENTATTI	IHNTBREOINA	LIEREDNTSFI	PBRPCSKEALA
OTEGLAHFRDY	IVNTNITOELA	ETRRNPUAICG	VEIGARNSLTE
UTIBLRSTEEF	CSUELOSHOOH	GELWRORASSK	IITPNONPING
IDEACRTROIN	EDINRLOAATC	TAGRSAMSTPI	TSOTSCIIHIR
ANIONIRTIGG	FCLOEYAABMN	LGYAAHPLRIC	BIEARPELRAR
WETGDNRAOUR	MREMSAKRYRE	AFYTAMGRREN	NRSEEROOFTH
OEERSHNSEGU	GIWANNDHTIR	SOIGOHAELNT	ENAESETISTC
AMVERHOTERS	SHLHREEWAIC	URAQBEKACTR	CAISSEEOSRC
CLLDITRAASY	ETIYRPLAORM	ATELONRSRAT	UCIGNMNAITL
BKOESNETLTC	ACDSECEOELN	NVOREASNBAI	SLDINITAVOA
YOMHRHCPITE	NITAIUIMLOH	FRLESUOUERC	OCKWBNIRAET
XEAENMETTRI	STRDEEUTLMK	AIIFRIYMTLA	PSRMOEKEMJU
TIGOLAIDOSR	ILNTMNEOATA	REEODCAALLT	ETHCRWNIKAE
EASEVGILTIL	RAVPPPROEAL	SPCYRROGTEO	IESCEGREMEN
OSIBIVERHAT	YITNEEADMRS	OTALRDAMUNS	SHIUGRNFINS
OCIERTLNECS	NITINRAUIFG	DRSLELUIATT	DSOCEARIDGU
AREIERCKEBS	DSRAERAEIVS	EFAMRENROCP	ADAPOEDDRLB
EGTANMIAIVI	ACSNISSRTIS	HTOLSIGUESH	OLTHEIITISS
ANISLUPTECG	UNLMEARTARI	ETIUCTDOANS	ALEEIRBNOCT
EPPRKCEEEEA	ARPMOSCCIOC	EFSSAETLRID	BLEAMSTONIH
NFOWSRMATEC	ALISTOGINBA	GCUONGANEIR	YSITLTABOEN
ALDGDLRLEBA	ADIDMEGYNRA	WAFRMSTNADO	SYCSRPAKSER
DAICLTIAELC	ELVECNEBENO	AGESEEREKPT	NRECELHGALS

Twelve Letters

OSIIDUCNJTRI	IAILLISBMUNG	TAGRRAELDEEH	ILRDOADPLSNH
ARETTUDNEJSM	NLGHIIHGHTGI	AKGRINABEJIL	RSYOONEHMENO
RRTTEHEMOSME	ELODIASCTARN	ECTAHNRGSTCA	AEEFGCCIIMNN
ALIGTAGLNIVN	GSNIIONEMSAK	NNUEOINCDTAI	ELTUECGFNLYL
ASIETIGRTPLN	TVTTUIAAQIEN	EILUGERSLSAT	NTOOATANMCNB
AHFENECKRHID	ENDIEGNRKRAT	UOIPLIRYACSC	SILUINRCOJTA
LIBLTGEYLIII	RRAKLWOLFESO	ESSEROAHLDLE	ANSEISSLSPEN
BRIATINBAEVO	LGHGAIENSNTI	ACIALEDYCALM	BTGELNATROII
NIETHXILAGRA	AKIJTGGCHLIN	ICOTAPHEGNHR	IIELTLEISLGA
ICEEEGLRBNEL	AROFIASBTICN	LAIHTMCYEAPL	RNASMRBSEIGA
ANLMAIYGCETL	HETNZMAEATAI	SSEOSCMIHNKE	NELLLVEYAMTO
ESTRENARFTII	CTGECNALRAIE	DEIQCSUIEATN	ESGARINFRDNE
PIOSHIANCHPM	NAYALBMYLFTO	HYNPLNEAOEDD	DAIITZNEALIO
TIVGETASENII	ANEETINLBNCI	GSIAEALNMCNI	CLISAOTEEINR
OTBMIAURSCUN	LSOAICNYOACL	HEHRTFOTAUOG	PATDIPREPORA
SEUCFOLSFNRE	OLZIIIANCTVI	NHGACOEROPYA	ISAAIRTTOCCR
AASTRERIUBTB	EROALIZRNITA	NABTORIDCGAS	FCSIFENCEEII
ALOPTICAGLOE	APKNELITOCMA	MNUEACERONLT	CODESINBEEDI
SDBYIETKSROA	AERAETRREHKB	ANHPSRSIUTBE	NDEDEOCCYNPE
BESOIISJVCTT	DUYTOLOARISL	TIRRCEABSANT	LLIFTBIEEDAR
VIMTNAIPUELA	UEOITSONTSAT	SMBLALIIEILR	AKIBKEGCABRN
IOOSTTENRNAI	GNOARERSCSEM	AAHRMUININTA	UHKREBSEOERA
AEIGAEGNXGRT	ALENPISIPCLR	ESTRLIZCASYL	EERIDBDAANDL
NMHCENTESTAN	ROWTHLTYABTE	GYELCTLIIMIA	IDLNGHDSALNO
AOILRTSBORAE	ADSOIRRBASEL	OERSAULIMHDN	PEIASCOKDELO
ONUAITIMTNLR	LCTSAILHYIOR	NSFIUROTRSAT	IEGOENRBHNSR
TROMAEEDSTNS	ANDSEROIJIGP	ESTCNASTSSLE	ABESATIRRNES
ESRELTRSTIRA	ETTCTORIHMSA	NSLSBLOGGWAI	RYIIINADPCSL
KTRREUBSQAAC	CSETEIONGITS	OLRTAEILONCA	NGIIAMOINSAT
YLOEETCSLETR	LCEJAALMYIST	AEISKAGFCCRN	TEIBNMLAYLVA
OCIGNFWNRDUD	NKSSEIDEILNS	AESSRTMIHGNN	ITASNRESBOOV
LSIENIATMTSO	EDERRATOSHCT	STAIACNPLSSD	EGTDAHAERTER
LTINAANEMAIB	AREHSESISDRR	AISENKTLSCCD	NGSRNDIFTEEA
MEDFEIHIDIRU	APPSAEENNRWM	ISBONAMNCITO	NMRRTAUEAFCU
OTCONPNMNILA	LFNSMLFTUILE	ASCSRIIISNTC	ENSICSESVDEI
ITIOAOPLEGCL	OILSCCOAITCN	KSHEBACLETAR	IRGSAUHDIPAN
TYDLIRSBTOOH	LYUROUSGITAT	SDAEGTITINER	AISTMNTNALOE
PLROACSSSHHI	LTFNIDIEIAEB	TEINNMLOYTPO	ESCRSUAFGNLE
KGCLNAAMBLII	OTMRIONFSAUL	AASCUTYLOMIL	LGTIHEFYDULL
ILEOCZAINFIT	ESCCORHSHDAT	LIIGAIUNLMNT	ITURTCASAPSH

Notes

Chapter 1

1 Lonergan's principal work, his study of the structure of human understanding, is *Insight*. Other significant philosophical works include *Understanding and Being, Phenomenology and Logic, Philosophical and Theological Papers 1958–1964,* and *Philosophical and Theological Papers 1965–1980*. Secondary works that provide helpful introductions to Lonergan include Byrne, *The Ethics of Discernment*; Flanagan, *Quest for Self-Knowledge*; Mathews, *Lonergan's Quest*; Meynell, *Introduction to the Philosophy of Bernard Lonergan*; and Melchin, *Living with Other People*. For secondary works that situate Lonergan within wider conversations in philosophy, see McCarthy, *The Crisis of Philosophy*; Fitzpatrick, *Philosophical Encounters*; Crysdale, ed., *Lonergan and Feminism*; Meynell, *Redirecting Philosophy*; Braman, *Meaning and Authenticity*. Lonergan's principal contribution to theology is *Method in Theology*. His most explicit discussion of the relevance of his cognitional theory to the field of education and learning is *Topics in Education*.

2 Some examples of my early work give you an idea of how I was thinking about Lonergan. See Melchin, *History, Ethics, and Emergent Probability*, "Ethics in *Insight*," and "History, Ethics, and Emergent Probability."

3 In the years prior, I had learned a few things from a Lonergan scholar who influenced me significantly, Philip McShane. What I learned from Phil prepared me for this new way of thinking about myself. See Melchin, "Exploring the Idea of Private Property," "Learning the Practice of Understanding Myself."

4 At this point I began understanding more fully the extent to which Insight studies is not merely an academic project but also a personal life project.

5 On the topics of "consciousness," Lonergan's method of "self-appropriation," and the role of questioning and wonder in the operations of consciousness, see, e.g., McShane, *Wealth of Self and Wealth of Nations*; Lonergan, *Method in Theology*, 8–22, and "Cognitive Structure."
6 In his book *The Ethics of Discernment*, Patrick Byrne uses the term "discernment" to speak about this heightened ability to observe, understand, and judge that arises from practice and skill development in a field of experience. For Byrne, however, the term has an additional meaning, and this is the meaning associated with understanding and taking responsibility for the operations of consciousness that we employ in all fields of experience. See, in particular, 14–17.
7 Two places where Lonergan explains "cognitional operations" are Lonergan, *Method in Theology*, 8–22, and "Cognitional Structure," 205–11.
8 For analyses of how feelings of threat constrict and distort parties' operations of understanding in conflict, see Melchin and Picard, *Transforming Conflict*, 78–90; Picard, *Practising Insight Mediation*, 15–25; Price and Melchin, *Spiritualizing Politics*, 95–100.
9 For a sampling of texts that illustrate the various ways democracy has been understood, see, e.g., MacPherson, *The Real World of Democracy*; Elshtain, *Democracy on Trial*; Benhabib, ed., *Democracy and Difference*; Sandel, *Democracy's Discontent*; Kaplan, "Was Democracy Just a Moment?"; Bohman and Rehg, eds., *Deliberative Democracy*; Kraynak, *Christian Faith and Modern Democracy*.
10 See, e.g., Wolin, "Fugitive Democracy," 31–3, 42; Hobbes, *Leviathan*, chapters 14–15.
11 For presentations of insights I gained more recently and resources I consulted, see Melchin, "Reaching Toward Democracy," "What is a Democracy Anyway?" and "Democracy and the Transformation of Conflict." Throughout this discussion, I draw upon the analysis of relevant voices as presented in Melchin, "Democracy and the Transformation of Conflict."
12 Melchin, "Democracy and the Transformation of Conflict," 103.
13 If you are questioning my use of the expression "reliable values," I offer, as evidence, your own act of questioning. Clearly you find this act to be reliable and valuable.
14 Melchin, "Democracy and the Transformation of Conflict," 104–5.
15 See, e.g., Rehg, *Insight and Solidarity*. The subtitle of Rehg's book is *The Discourse Ethics of Jürgen Habermas*.
16 Taylor, "The Politics of Recognition," 70; see also Melchin, "Democracy and the Transformation of Conflict," 105–6.
17 Hollenbach uses the language of "learning" to speak about this transformation that goes on in democratic discourse. See, Hollenbach, *The Common Good and Christian Ethics*, 138.
18 Taylor, "The Politics of Recognition," 67, 70–3. For an excellent analysis of Taylor and Lonergan, see Braman, *Meaning and Authenticity*.

19 For an approach to conflict that places Lonergan's approach to "learning about learning" at the centre of conflict analysis and mediation, see Melchin and Picard, *Transforming Conflict*, chapters 3 and 4.
20 See Grallo, *Question and Insight in Everyday Life*, chapter 3.
21 For a technical account of these and other features of scientific explanation, see Lonergan, *Insight*, 61–7.
22 Mark Morelli uses the expression "performative self-contradiction" to speak about this strange way we often contradict ourselves. "The contradiction in performative self-contradiction is between what I'm saying and my performance in saying it." Morelli, *Self-Possession*, 19. For more on this topic, see the discussions of Byrne and Morelli in chapter 5.
23 See Byrne, *The Ethics of Discernment*, chapters 1–3 for an excellent explanation of self-appropriation.
24 This is the approach taken by Lonergan in, e.g., *Insight*, 12–15.
25 This is the approach taken by Byrne in *The Ethics of Discernment*, 99–101, 156–60, 184–91, 243–4, and elsewhere. Byrne, Morelli, and McShane also follow Lonergan in inviting readers to identify the operations in their own consciousness.
26 This is the approach taken by Morelli in *Self-Possession*, 1–7.
27 This is the approach taken by McShane in *Wealth of Self and Wealth of Nations*, chapter 3.
28 I suggest three websites where readers may find help in identifying coaches or mentors: The Lonergan Institute, Boston College, https://www.bc.edu/bc-web/academics/sites/the-lonergan-institute.html; Insight Today, https://www.insighttodayonline.com/; and Insight Collaborations Institute, https://www.insightcollaborations.org/.
29 For lists of texts for further reading, see chapter 1, note 1; chapter 5, notes 1–51; and chapter 6, note 1.
30 For examples, see the names and texts of authors listed in the notes to chapter 5.

Chapter 2

1 If you look through the book *1000 Scramble Words* by Bryce Ross, you will find some three-letter words scattered throughout the pages.
2 I have found the following puzzle books to be helpful: Knurek and Hoyt, *Jumble Workout*; Knurek, Hoyt, Arnold, and Lee, *Jumble Symphony*; Ross, *1000 Word Scrambles*; VisCulture, *Word Scramble*.
3 For an account of the meaning of the expression, "self-appropriation," see Byrne, *The Ethics of Discernment*, 31–5, 74–92, 285–306. Morelli uses the term "self-possession" to speak about self-appropriation, see Morelli, *Self-Possession*, xi–xv.
4 In chapter 6 of her book *An Anatomy of Everyday Arguments*, 79–81, Marnie Jull provides a good example of this attention to questioning

in conversations. She is in a conversation with her friend, Gabriel, and readers can observe how she pays close attention to his meaning, asking further questions to gain a better understanding of what he is trying to express. She treats the conversation like a puzzle, seeking ways of helping Gabriel figure out what is going on in his relationship with Felicity.

5 In the introduction to his book *Question and Insight in Everyday Life*, Richard Grallo outlines one of the aims of the book as "offer[ing] some guidance in self-management, allowing the reader to put this knowledge to use by better coordinating the mental events which enable human problem solving." He does not use the expression, "jump to conclusions." But in every chapter of the book, readers can observe how failure to coordinate mental events can lead to this type of problem arising in conversations.

6 In chapter 2 of her book *Practising Insight Mediation*, Cheryl Picard provides an account of how experiences of threat can derail conversations, shifting them away from cooperation and towards conflict. Her account is situated in relation to the process of mediation. But readers will find this account helpful for everyday conversations.

Chapter 3

1 Lonergan uses the expression "cognitional theory" to refer to a philosopher's explanation of our operations of cognition: the operations involved in experiencing, understanding, judging, and deciding. Lonergan's cognitional theory arises from the self-reflective empirical method of self-appropriation. This is the method you are learning in the practice modules of this book. In chapter 1 of *Method in Theology*, he discusses cognitional theory in the sub-section "Transcendental Method," 23–4. In an earlier essay, he uses the term "cognitional structure" to speak about the operations of experiencing, understanding, and judgment as they are explained in his cognitional theory; see Lonergan, "Cognitional Structure." See also Byrne's discussion of cognitional structure in *The Ethics of Discernment*, 41–55.

2 In *Method in Theology*, 18, Lonergan lists four groups of operations: experience, understanding, judgment, and decision. In his earlier essay, "Cognitional Structure," 206–7, he lists three groups of operations: experience, understanding, and judgment. In *The Ethics of Discernment*, 95–9, Byrne offers an explanation of this shift from three groups of operations to four.

3 See, e.g., Jamie Price, "Method in Analyzing Conflict Behavior"; Jull, *An Anatomy of Everyday Arguments*, 157–60.

4 For an example of this approach, see Melchin, *Living with Other People*, 17–27.

5 I am grateful to Michael Payette for offering this suggestion.

6 Grallo offers examples of this practical, problem-solving mode of engaging our cognitional operations in *Question and Insight in Everyday Life*, 31, 37–8. Morelli offers an account of this practical mode (he uses the term "motif") in *Self-Possession*, 196–206.

Chapter 4

1 See Melchin, *Living with Other People*, 17–27. Byrne offers a detailed overview of the operations involved in raising and answering questions of value, decision, and action in *The Ethics of Discernment*, chapter 4.
2 See Byrne's excellent analysis of the role of feelings in raising and answering questions of value, decision, and action in *The Ethics of Discernment*, chapters 5–9.
3 See Morelli's presentation in *Self-Possession*, chapter 1. See also Lonergan, *Method in Theology*, 35–7, and Byrne, *The Ethics of Discernment*, 416–21, 426.
4 See Grallo, *Question and Insight in Everyday Life*, chapter 1, particularly 23–7.
5 See, e.g., Grallo, *Question and Insight in Everyday Life*, 31, 37–8, and Melchin, *Living with Other People*, 17–27.
6 See, e.g., Jull, *An Anatomy of Everyday Arguments*, 26–8, 96–7, and Picard, *Practising Insight Mediation*, 15–25.
7 Megan Price provides an excellent example of a training program for police based on the Insight approach. Law enforcement professionals are trained to observe their own cognitional operations and feelings of threat and to implement strategies for deliberately asking questions that can de-escalate stressful situations. See Megan Price, "The Process and Partnerships behind Insight Policing."

Chapter 5

1 For examples of works that apply resources from Lonergan to economics, see the essays in Liddy, ed., "Forging a New Economic Paradigm." For contributions to business, see, e.g., Ahner, *Business Ethics*; Little, "Mind – Your Own Business," "Trust in Business"; McAleese, "From Abstract Catholic Social Thought"; Melchin, "What is 'The Good' of Business"; Stebbins, "Business, Faith and the Common Good," "The Meaning of Solidarity." For contributions to physics and evolutionary science, see, e.g., Byrne, "Lonergan and the Foundations of the Theories of Relativity"; Flanagan, "From Body to Thing," "*Insight*: Chapters 1–5"; Ogilvie, "Charles Darwin, 140 Years On." For contributions to environmental studies, see, e.g., Byrne, *Toward Environmental Wholeness*; McAuley, "Unfolding Eco-Climate Crisis." For contributions to urban studies, see, e.g., Kidder, "The Future of American Cities," "Lonergan, Liberalism, and the Good of Cities." For contributions to nursing, see, e.g., Belair, "The Contribution

of the Nurse to the Human Good"; Perry, "Self-Transcendence." For contributions to education, see, e.g., Fitzpatrick, "Bernard Lonergan: Educationist and Philosopher"; Gilbert, "A Lonerganian Critique"; Guasti, "Method and the Curriculum"; Tackney, "General Empirical Method."

2 Byrne, *The Ethics of Discernment.*
3 See chapter 1 for his discussion of discernment and self-appropriation.
4 Chapters 5–9 deal with the role of feelings in ethics.
5 See the Introduction and chapter 1.
6 Byrne begins his treatment of the fundamental role of questioning in responsible judgments in his discussion of factual knowing in chapter 2, pages 52–5. He continues this treatment in ethical intentionality in chapter 4, pages 104–9. And readers can observe the centrality of this focus on the fundamental role of questioning throughout the chapters of the book.
7 See these discussions in chapters 7–9.
8 See these discussions in chapters 13 and 14.
9 For an application of this method to the field of environmental ethics, see Byrne, *Toward Environmental Wholeness.*
10 Byrne, *The Ethics of Discernment,* 436.
11 Melchin and Picard, *Transforming Conflict.* See also Picard, *Practising Insight Mediation.*
12 For an overview of theories and approaches to conflict and mediation see Melchin and Picard, *Transforming Conflict,* chapter 2.
13 See the discussion of the approach of Fisher and Ury in Melchin and Picard, *Transforming Conflict,* 43–6.
14 See the discussion of the approach of Bush and Folger in Melchin and Picard, *Transforming Conflict,* 43–6.
15 For lists of some of the published works that draw on the Insight approach to conflict, see the Bibliographies in Jamie Price, *The Call*; Price and Melchin, *Spiritualizing Politics*; and Picard, *Practising Insight Mediation,* particularly the works by Alfani, Bartoli, Jull, Melchin, Peddle, Picard, Jamie Price, Megan Price, and Price and Obasi.
16 On conflict as learning, see *Transforming Conflict,* 18–24, 46–8, 83–4.
17 On the role of threat in conflict, see Picard, *Practising Insight Mediation,* chapter 2, especially pages 15–25.
18 "Deepening" is the most important part of the mediation process. See Picard, *Practising Insight Mediation,* 79–93, 126–34.
19 For a discussion of Lonergan's analysis of feelings and values in the Insight approach to conflict, see Picard, *Practising Insight Mediation,* 44–47; Melchin and Picard, *Transforming Conflict,* 70–75 and 84–90.
20 Jull, *An Anatomy of Everyday Arguments.*
21 Jull, *An Anatomy of Everyday Arguments,* 11.
22 See chapter 1 for her presentation of autoethnography. See also pages 40–1.

23 On the role of the Insight approach in her analysis, with its focus on the role of threats in conflict, see pages 7–8, 18, 26–8, 104–6, 126–9, 136–7, 141–2.
24 Jull, *An Anatomy of Everyday Arguments*, 38–9.
25 For discussions that draw on Lonergan's explanation of operations of consciousness for her sociological analysis, see 21–2, 31, 46, 50, 78, 102–3, 117–18, 125–6, 144.
26 Grallo, *Question and Insight in Everyday Life*.
27 See his Introduction, pages 1–3.
28 Grallo, *Question and Insight in Everyday Life*, 2.
29 Grallo, *Question and Insight in Everyday Life*, 49.
30 For his discussion of the "patterns" of problem solving, see 15–20.
31 Grallo, *Question and Insight in Everyday Life*, 16.
32 Grallo, *Question and Insight in Everyday Life*, 139.
33 Morelli, *Self-Possession*.
34 On the various motifs, see chapters 6–12, pages 173–256.
35 See the final section of each motif chapter, 204–6, 215–18, 226, 234–6, 247–8.
36 The meditations are found throughout the chapters. See, e.g., 9, 10, 21–2, 24–5, 35–6, 42, 69–70, 76, 91–4. There are many more.
37 Morelli, *Self-Possession*, 21–2.
38 Morelli, *Self-Possession*, 18.
39 Morelli, *Self-Possession*, 19, italics in the original.
40 Morelli, *Self-Possession*, 18–19, see also 10–11.
41 Jamie Price, *The Call*.
42 For background information, see the Introduction, xi–xix, and the Preface to Price and Melchin, *Spiritualizing Politics*, ix–xii.
43 Jamie Price, *The Call*, xi.
44 See Price and Melchin, *Spiritualizing Politics*, 10. Chapter 1 of this book provides an overview of key features of Shriver's approach to spirituality and politics.
45 Jamie Price, *The Call*, 55.
46 This comes to fruition in Conversation 9, pages 204–30.
47 The model is discussed in the narrative and explained most fully in the notes to Conversations 3, 4, and 5. In Conversations 8 and 9, readers observe the model being applied in the dialogue.
48 Shriver uses the expression "spontaneous combustion" on page 207.
49 The roleplay begins on page 211 and continues to near the end of the Conversation.
50 Discussions and analyses of Shriver's work combatting racism in Chicago can be found in Conversations 4, 5, 6, and 8, and elsewhere.
51 On the universality of the model, see the discussion in note 14, page 264. The reference is to page 104 of the dialogue.

Chapter 6

1 For examples of published works that draw on Lonergan for analyses of Christian colleges and universities, see Haughey, *Where Is Knowing Going?*; Snell and Cone, *Authentic Cosmopolitanism*.

Bibliography

Sample Scramble Word Puzzle Books

Knurek, Jeff, and David Hoyt. *Jumble Workout: Puzzles to Make Your Heart Race!* Chicago: Triumph Books, 2014. https://www.triumphbooks.com/jumble–workout-products-9781600789434.php?page_id=95.

Knurek, Jeff, David Hoyt, Henri Arnold, and Bob Lee. *Jumble Symphony: An Orchestra of Perplexing Puzzles!* Chicago: Triumph Books, 2015. https://www.triumphbooks.com/jumble–symphony-products-9781629371313.php?page_id=95.

Ross, Bryce. *1000 Word Scrambles: A Jumble of Fun for All Levels*. Bolton, ON: Puzzle Pals/Amazon, 2019. https://www.amazon.ca/1000-WORD-SCRAMBLES-Jumble-Levels/dp/1709033029.

VisCulture Publishing. *Word Scramble: 2000 Jumbled Words 50 Unique Themes*. Bolton, ON: VisCulture Publishing/Amazon, 2021. https://www.amazon.ca/Word-Scramble-Jumbled-Unique-Themes/dp/B09B5HYH42/ref=sr_1_1?qid=1704475362&refinements=p_27%3AVisCulture+Publishing&s=books&sr=1-1.

Works Cited

Ahner, Gene. *Business Ethics: Making a Life, Not Just a Living*. Maryknoll, NY: Orbis Books, 2007.

Belair, Jean. "The Contribution of the Nurse to the Human Good." In *Lonergan Workshop* Vol. 14, edited by Fred Lawrence, 1–57. Chestnut Hill, MA: Boston College, 1998.

Benhabib, Seyla, ed. *Democracy and Difference: Contesting the Boundaries of the Political*. Princeton: Princeton University Press, 1996.

Braman, Brian. *Meaning and Authenticity: Bernard Lonergan and Charles Taylor on the Drama of Authentic Human Existence.* Toronto: University of Toronto Press, 2008.

Bohman, James, and William Rehg, eds. *Deliberative Democracy: Essays on Reason and Politics.* Cambridge, MA: MIT Press, 1997.

Byrne, Patrick. *The Ethics of Discernment: Lonergan's Foundations for Ethics.* Toronto: University of Toronto Press, 2016.

– "Lonergan and the Foundations of the Theories of Relativity." In *Creativity and Method*, edited by Matthew Lamb, 477–94. Milwaukee: Marquette University Press, 1981.

– *Toward Environmental Wholeness: Method in Environmental Ethics and Science.* Albany, NY: SUNY Press, 2024.

Crysdale, Cynthia, ed. *Lonergan and Feminism.* Toronto: University of Toronto Press, 1994.

Elshtain, Jean Bethke. *Democracy on Trial.* Concord, ON: Anansi Press, 1993.

Fitzpatrick, Joseph. "Bernard Lonergan: Educationist and Philosopher." In *Lonergan Workshop* Vol. 17, edited by Fred Lawrence, 85–94. Chestnut Hill, MA: Boston College, 2002.

– *Philosophical Encounters: Lonergan and the Analytic Tradition.* Toronto: University of Toronto Press, 2005.

Flanagan, Joseph. "From Body to Thing." In *Creativity and Method*, edited by Matthew Lamb, 495–507. Milwaukee: Marquette University Press, 1981.

– "*Insight*: Chapters 1–5." In *Lonergan Workshop* Vol. 8, edited by Fred Lawrence, 85–107. Atlanta: Scholars Press, 1990.

– *Quest for Self-Knowledge: An Essay in Lonergan's Philosophy.* Toronto: University of Toronto Press, 1997.

Gilbert, Christopher. "A Lonerganian Critique of the Pragmatic Method of Education." *METHOD: Journal of Lonergan Studies* 11, no. 2 (1993): 199–214.

Grallo, Richard. *Question and Insight in Everyday Life: A Blueprint for Transformative Problem Solving.* Lanham, MD: Lexington Books, 2022.

Guasti, Lucio. "Method and the Curriculum." *The Lonergan Review* 1, no. 1 (Spring 2009): 11–29.

Haughey, John. *Where Is Knowing Going? The Horizons of the Knowing Subject.* Washington: Georgetown University Press, 2009.

Hobbes, Thomas. *Leviathan.* Edited by Michael Oakeshott. New York: Collier Books, 1977.

Hollenbach, David. *The Common Good and Christian Ethics.* Cambridge: Cambridge University Press, 2002.

Jull, Marnie. *An Anatomy of Everyday Arguments: Conflict and Change through Insight.* Montreal: McGill-Queen's University Press, 2022.

Kaplan, Robert D. "Was Democracy Just a Moment?" *The Atlantic Monthly* 280 (December 1997): 55–60.

Kidder, Paul. "The Future of American Cities." In *Lonergan Workshop* Vol. 17, edited by Fred Lawrence, 125–41. Chestnut Hill, MA: Boston College, 2002.

- "Lonergan, Liberalism, and the Good of Cities." *Theoforum* 45, no. 1 (2014): 81–99.
Kraynak, Robert. *Christian Faith and Modern Democracy.* Notre Dame: University of Notre Dame Press, 2001.
Liddy, Richard M., ed. "Forging a New Economic Paradigm: Perspectives from Bernard Lonergan." *The Lonergan Review* 2, no. 1 (Spring 2010): 1–382.
Little, John. "Mind – Your Own Business." In *Australian Lonergan Workshop* Vol. 2, edited by Matthew Ogilvie and William Danaher, 48–60. Sydney: Novum Organum Press, 2002.
- "Trust in Business." *Theoforum* 43, no. 1–2 (2012): 47–68.
Lonergan, Bernard. "Cognitional Structure." In *Collection*, Vol. 4 of *Collected Works of Bernard Lonergan*, edited by Frederick Crowe and Robert Doran, 2nd ed., 205–21. Toronto: University of Toronto Press, 1993.
- *Insight: A Study of Human Understanding.* Vol. 3 of *Collected Works of Bernard Lonergan*, edited by Frederick Crowe and Robert Doran, 5th ed. Toronto: University of Toronto Press, 1992.
- *Method in Theology.* Vol. 14 of *Collected Works of Bernard Lonergan*, edited by Robert Doran and John Dadosky, 2nd ed. Toronto: University of Toronto Press, 2017.
- *Phenomenology and Logic.* Vol. 18 of *Collected Works of Bernard Lonergan*, edited by Philip McShane. Toronto: University of Toronto Press, 2001.
- *Philosophical and Theological Papers 1958–1964.* Vol. 6 of *Collected Works of Bernard Lonergan*, edited by Robert Croken, Frederick Crowe, and Robert Doran. Toronto: University of Toronto Press, 1996.
- *Philosophical and Theological Papers 1965–1980.* Vol. 17 of *Collected Works of Bernard Lonergan*, edited by Robert Croken and Robert Doran. Toronto: University of Toronto Press, 2004.
- *Topics in Education.* Vol. 10 of *Collected Works of Bernard Lonergan*, edited by Frederick Crowe. Toronto: University of Toronto Press, 1993.
- *Understanding and Being.* Vol. 5 of *Collected Works of Bernard Lonergan*, edited by Frederick Crowe, Robert Doran, Thomas Daly, Elizabeth Morelli, and Mark Morelli, 2nd ed. Toronto: University of Toronto Press, 1990.
MacPherson, Crawford B. *The Real World of Democracy.* Concord, ON: Anansi Press, 1992.
Mathews, William. *Lonergan's Quest.* Toronto: University of Toronto Press, 2005.
McAleese, Morag. "From Abstract Catholic Social Thought Principles to the Concrete in the Common Good Model of Business." *Theoforum* 43, no. 1–2 (2012): 85–106.
McAuley, Thomas. "Unfolding Eco-Climate Crisis: And the Universe as Emergently Probable." In *Lonergan's Anthropology Revisited: The Next Fifty Years of Vatican II*, edited by Gerard Whelan, 475–8. Rome: Gregorian & Biblical Press, 2015.
McCarthy, Michael. *The Crisis of Philosophy.* Albany: SUNY Press, 1989.

McShane, Philip. *Wealth of Self and Wealth of Nations*. 2nd ed., edited by James Duffy. Vancouver: Axial Publishing, 2021.

Melchin, Kenneth. "Democracy and the Transformation of Conflict: Ideas from Bernard Lonergan." *Theoforum* 45, no. 1 (2014): 101–18.

– "Ethics in *Insight*." In *Lonergan Workshop* Vol. 8, edited by Fred Lawrence, 135–47. Atlanta: Scholars Press, 1990.

– "Exploring the Idea of Private Property: A Small Step along the Road from Common Sense to Theory." *Journal of Macrodynamic Analysis* 3 (2003): 287–301.

– *History, Ethics, and Emergent Probability*. 2nd ed. Ottawa: The Lonergan Website, 1999.

– "History, Ethics, and Emergent Probability." In *Lonergan Workshop* Vol. 7, edited by Fred Lawrence, 269–94. Atlanta: Scholars Press, 1988.

– "Learning the Practice of Understanding Myself." *Journal of Macrodynamic Analysis* 15 (2022): 111–15.

– *Living with Other People*. Ottawa: Novalis, 1998.

– "Reaching Toward Democracy: Theology and Theory When Talk Turns to War." *Catholic Theological Society of America, Proceedings* 58 (2003): 41–59.

– "What is a Democracy Anyway? A Discussion between Lonergan and Rawls." In *Lonergan Workshop* Vol. 15, edited by Fred Lawrence, 99–116. Chestnut Hill, MA: Boston College, 1999.

– "What is 'The Good' of Business? Insights from the Work of Bernard Lonergan." *Anglican Theological Review* 87, no. 1 (2005): 43–61.

Melchin, Kenneth, and Cheryl Picard. *Transforming Conflict through Insight*. Toronto: University of Toronto Press, 2008.

Meynell, Hugo. *Introduction to the Philosophy of Bernard Lonergan*. 2nd ed. Toronto: University of Toronto Press, 1991.

– *Redirecting Philosophy: Reflections on the Nature of Knowledge from Plato to Lonergan*. Toronto: University of Toronto Press, 1998.

Morelli, Mark. *Self-Possession: Being at Home in Conscious Performance*. 2nd ed. Los Angeles: Encanto Editions, 2019.

Ogilvie, Matthew. "Charles Darwin, 140 Years On: A Work in Progress/Evolution." In *Australian Lonergan Workshop II*, edited by Matthew Ogilvie and William Danaher, 201–12. Sydney: Novum Organum Press, 2002.

Perry, Donna J. "Self-Transcendence: Lonergan's Key to Integration of Nursing Theory, Research, and Practice." *Nursing Philosophy* 5, no. 1 (2004): 67–74.

Picard, Cheryl. *Practising Insight Mediation*. Toronto: University of Toronto Press, 2016.

Price, Jamie. *The Call: The Spiritual Realism of Sargent Shriver*. Los Angeles: SSPI Press, 2023.

– "Method in Analyzing Conflict Behavior: The Insight Approach." *Revista de Mediación* 11, no. 1 (2018): 1–9.

Price, James, and Kenneth Melchin. *Spiritualizing Politics without Politicizing Religion: The Example of Sargent Shriver*. Toronto: University of Toronto Press, 2022.

Price, Megan. "The Process and Partnerships behind Insight Policing." *Criminal Justice Policy Review* 27, no. 5 (2016): 553–67.

Rehg, William. *Insight and Solidarity: The Discourse Ethics of Jürgen Habermas*. Berkeley: University of California Press, 1997.

Sandel, Michael. *Democracy's Discontent: America in Search of a Public Philosophy*. Cambridge, MA: Harvard University Press, 1996.

Snell, R.J., and Steven Cone. *Authentic Cosmopolitanism: Love, Sin, and Grace in the Christian University*. Eugene, OR: Pickwick Publications, 2013.

Stebbins, J. Michael. "Business, Faith and the Common Good." *Review of Business* 19 (1997): 5–8.

– "The Meaning of Solidarity." In *Labor, Solidarity and the Common Good: Essays on the Ethical Foundations of Management*, edited by S.A. Cortright, 61–74. Durham, NC: Carolina Academic Press, 2001.

Tackney, Charles T. "General Empirical Method and the European Higher Education Area." In *Lonergan's Anthropology Revisited: The Next Fifty Years of Vatican II*, edited by Gerard Whelan, 491–4. Rome: Gregorian & Biblical Press, 2015.

Taylor, Charles. "The Politics of Recognition." In *Multiculturalism: Examining the Politics of Recognition*, edited by Amy Gutmann, 25–73. Princeton: Princeton University Press, 1994.

Wolin, Sheldon S. "Fugitive Democracy." In *Democracy and Difference*, edited by Seyla Benhabib, 31–45. Princeton: Princeton University Press, 1996.

Index

action: decision and, 55, 67, 70–1, 75, 81–2, 99; questioning about, 55. *See also* decision
applying the skills, 43–5, 63–4, 79–82. *See also* everyday life
arguments, everyday, 93–5
Aristotle, 85
attention, dividing and shifting, 32, 38, 42–3, 56
autoethnography, 93–4

Bush, Robert Baruch, 90
Byrne, Patrick, 20, 70, 72, 85–8, 120n6, 124n6

cars, 15
city living, limitations of, 4, 6
cognition, 122n1
competition (feeling), 66
competitive pressure, 32, 42–3, 49, 51–2, 59, 62; exploring feelings of, 65–9, 71–9. *See also* puzzle solving
concentration, 47
conflict, 89–94
consciousness: motifs, 99; objects of, 37, 39, 100; operations of, 53, 120nn5–6, 125n25; patterns, 96–7; philosophy and, 98–9

contradiction, 100, 121n22. *See also* self-contradiction
conversations, 44, 63–4
critical thinking: examples of, 7; Insight studies and, 8, 16–17; practicing, 7–8; self-knowledge and, 14–17, 106, 108

data, observing vs. describing, 54
decision, 14, 72–5, 81–2, 99; explaining the operation of, 55, 65–7, 70–2. *See also* action
democracy, 11–14, 106
direct insight, 18, 21, 25, 43, 46, 60–1, 63–4; conflict and, 91; differentiating the operation of, 47, 50; explaining the operation of, 53–6, 69–72; identifying the operation of, 56–9; questioning for, 62, 70; self-knowledge and, 37–8; values and, 65, 67, 79–80. *See also* insight; understanding
discernment, 85–8, 120n6

empiricism, 38
ethics, 84–8
ethnography, auto-, 93–4

everyday life: applying skills from Insight studies in, 43–5, 63–4, 79–82; direct insights in, 63; judgments in, 63
evidence, appeals to, 16, 86
experience, 54–5

facts, questioning about, 55
feelings: decisions and, 72–5; ethics and, 86; identifying, 66–9; for Lonergan, 92; mastery over, 32; noticing, 67; overview of, 65; puzzle solving and, 32, 66, 79; questioning and, 70–1; scramble word puzzles and, 66; values and, 70–5, 86
"figure out" (expression), 63
Fisher, Roger, 89
Folger, Joseph, 90

game shows, 63
Grallo, Richard, 14, 95–8, 107, 122n5, 123n6

Hollenbach, David, 120n17

Ignatius of Loyola, 85
incline, use of term, 73
insight: after-the-, 39, 58–9; before-the-, 39, 58–9, 91; conflict and, 89–93; judgment and, 80; Lonergan and, 91; reflective, 56, 60; verifying, 80. *See also* direct insight
Insight studies: as academic discipline, 22; benefits, 106–7; critical thinking and, 8, 16–17; defined, 3; democracy and, 11–14; music (compared to), 24; as practice, 8, 17, 23, 27, 79–82, 105; scramble word puzzles and, 27; self-knowledge and, 8, 14, 17
interest theory, 89–90

jokes, 63
judgment, 16, 21, 46, 63–4, 107; conflict and, 92; differentiating the operation of, 47–8, 50; ethics and, 84–8; explaining the operation of, 53–6, 69–72; identifying the operation of, 59–62; psychology and, 96–7; questioning for, 60, 72; self-knowledge and, 10, 13–14; values and, 65–6, 70–6, 79–82. *See also* verification
Jull, Marnie, 93–5, 107, 121n4
jumble word puzzles. *See* scramble word puzzles

knowing, theory of, 53–6, 69–72

listening, 10
Lonergan, Bernard: author's introduction to, 4; cognition for, 122n1; data of consciousness for, 38; economics (applications in), 123n1; ethics for, 87–8; feelings for, 92; inner normativity and, 76; insight and, 91; operations for, 55, 122n2; overview of works, 119n1; reception of work, 23; self-appropriation for, 16, 36, 120n5; self-knowledge and, 23, 83, 90–1; values for, 92

McShane, Philip, 119n3
mediation, 89–93
meditation(s), 32, 98, 100
mind, the: attention and, 32, 38; describing self-reflexively, 18–19; differences between others, 15; harm from, 3; inclining of, 73–4, 77–9; loops, 65, 71; normative behaviours, 17–18; observing, 40–2, 46–7, 57–9, 78–9; operations of, 36–43, 52, 62, 73, 76–7; questioning and, 55, 81; self-knowledge and, 10–11, 70; stretching, 17–18, 106–7; structure of, 47
Morelli, Mark, 98–100, 121n22
music, playing: cooperation and, 9–10; difficulty of learning, 38;

Insight studies compared to, 8, 17, 21, 24, 46, 51, 64, 105; self-knowledge and, 10

normativity, inner, 76–9, 85, 88, 100

object of consciousness, 37, 39, 52, 100
objectivity, 100
operations: direct insights and, 47, 54, 56–9, 70; groups of (differentiating), 47–53; of judgment, 60–2; judgments and, 55–6, 59–62; for Lonergan, 55, 122n2; loops of, 55–6, 65, 71; of the mind, 36–43, 52, 62, 73, 76–7; questioning and, 71–2; sensory, 54; understanding and, 55–6, 70; verification and, 48, 54–5, 72, 79, 82
organisms: inner structure, 6; self-organization, 6; thinking of ourselves as, 6, 107

patterns, 96–7
Paul of Tarsus, 85
peacebuilding, 103
performance anxiety, 32, 42–3, 49, 51–2, 59, 62; exploring feelings of, 65–9, 71–9. *See also* puzzle solving
personal, politics as, 13
philosophy, debate in, 11, 12–13
Picard, Cheryl, 89, 91, 93–4, 107, 122n6
politics, 101–3, 106; as personal, 13
positions and counter-positions, 87–8. *See also* self-contradiction
practice-based approach, 9, 14, 17–20
Price, Jamie, 101–3
Price, Megan, 123n7
problem-solving, 95–8
psychology, 95–8
puzzle solving: anxiety and, 27–8, 31, 35, 43, 49, 52, 59, 66–7, 74–5; applying skills from, 43–5; daily routine, 29–31; direct insight and, 57; feelings and, 32, 66, 79; instructions, 30–1, 33–5, 40–3, 49–51, 57–61, 68–9, 74–5; overview, 18, 19, 46; pausing during, 31–2, 37, 39, 40–2, 49–50, 53, 57, 79; self-knowledge and, 19, 79; special procedure for, 31–6. *See also* competitive pressure; performance anxiety; scramble word puzzles; self-esteem

questioning: about action, 55; conflict and, 91; in conversations, 121n4; direct insights and, 62; about fact, 55; judgment and, 60, 72; the mind and, 55, 81; noticing, 19–20, 44; operations and, 71–2; pausing leading to, 53; about value, 55; verification and, 60, 70

racism, 103
relationships, 8–9, 17, 43, 56, 104, 107; conflict and, 84, 90–2; psychology and, 97
reliable values, 12, 120n13

schools, 8–9, 17, 43
scramble word puzzles: comparing between, 67–9, 73–4, 77; creating your own, 28; difficulty levels of, 25–9, 35–6, 52, 67, 79; feelings and, 66; Insight studies and, 27; overview of, 24–5, 27; sources for, 121nn1–2; verification (questions for), 54–5, 60. *See also* puzzle solving
self-appropriation, 16, 36, 86–9, 94, 101
self-awareness, 104
self-contradiction, 100, 121n22. *See also* contradiction; positions and counter-positions
self-esteem, 32, 42–3, 47, 49, 51–2, 59, 62; exploring feelings of, 65–9, 71–9. *See also* puzzle solving

self-knowledge: application of, 83; benefits of, 13–14, 107–8; critical thinking and, 14–17, 106, 108; discernment and, 85; discomfort from, 13; Insight studies and, 8, 14, 17; Lonergan's work and, 23, 83, 90–1; mind and, 10–11, 70; music and, 10; as practice, 83; puzzle solving and, 19, 79; spirituality and, 102

self-possession, 98–100

self-transcendence, 103

self-understanding, 4

sensory operations, 54, 70

Shriver, Robert Sargent, 101–3, 125n44

skill development, 51–3, 56, 63–4, 67, 80

social media, 10, 106

sociology, 93–5, 107

spirituality, 101–3

Taylor, Charles, 13

threats, 82, 122n6

Transformative Mediation model, 90

truth, 100

understanding, 14, 18, 20, 25, 52, 60, 105; conflict and, 91; differentiating the operation of, 47, 48; ethics and, 85–6; explaining the operation of, 53–6, 69–72; identifying the operation of, 56–9; psychology and, 96; questioning for, 53–4, 70–3; self-knowledge and, 4, 8, 37, 39; values and, 81–2. *See also* direct insight

values: decisions and, 72–5; ethics and, 87; feelings and, 70–5, 86; identifying, 66–70; judgments and, 81, 86; for Lonergan, 92; questioning about, 55; reliable, 12, 120n13

verification, 7, 54–7, 61; conflict and, 92; differentiating the operation of, 48; explaining the operation of, 53–6, 69–72; identifying the operation of, 59–62; questioning for, 60, 70; self-knowledge and, 39; values and, 72, 81–2. *See also* judgment

word puzzles. *See* scramble word puzzles

workplaces, 8–9, 17, 43, 97

www.ingramcontent.com/pod-product-compliance
Ingram Content Group UK Ltd.
Pitfield, Milton Keynes, MK11 3LW, UK
UKHW021626090925
462704UK00014B/76/J